CLIFFSCOMPLETE

Shakespeare's

Julius Caesar

Edited by Sidney Lamb

Associate Professor of English

Sir George Williams University, Montreal

Complete Text + Commentary + Glossary

Commentary by Diana Sweeney

IDG Books Worldwide, Inc.

An International Data Group Company

Foster City, CA • Chicago, IL • Indianapolis, IN • New York, NY

CLIFFSCOMPLETE

Shakespeare's

Julius Caesar

About the Author

Diana Sweeney has an M.A. from The Shakespeare Institute in Stratford-upon-Avon. She has both taught and directed Shakespeare for the past fifteen years at North Hollywood High School in Los Angeles, California.

Publisher's Acknowledgments

Editorial

Project Editor: Elizabeth Netedu Kuball

Acquisitions Editor: Gregory W. Tubach

Editorial Director: Kristin A. Cocks

Special Help: Michelle Hacker

Production

Indexer: Rebecca R. Plunkett

Proofreader: Christine Pingleton

IDG Books Indianapolis Production Department

CliffsComplete Julius Caesar

Published by

IDG Books Worldwide, Inc.

An International Data Group Company

919 E. Hillsdale Blvd.

Suite 400

Foster City, CA 94404

www.idgbooks.com (IDG Books Worldwide Web site)

www.cliffsnotes.com (CliffsNotes Web site)

Library of Congress Control No.: 00-101107

ISBN: 0-7645-8569-X

Printed in the United States of America

10 9 8 7 6 5 4 3 2 1

1O/RT/QU/QQ/IN

Distributed in the United States by IDG Books Worldwide, Inc.

Distributed by CDG Books Canada Inc. for Canada; by Transworld Publishers Limited in the United Kingdom; by IDG Norge Books for Norway; by IDG Sweden Books for Sweden; by IDG Books Australia Publishing Corporation Pty. Ltd. for Australia and New Zealand; by TransQuest Publishers Pte Ltd. for Singapore, Malaysia, Thailand, Indonesia, and Hong Kong; by Gotop Information Inc. for Taiwan; by ICG Muse, Inc. for Japan; by Intersoft for South Africa; by Eyrolles for France; by International Thomson Publishing for Germany, Austria and Switzerland; by Distribuidora Cuspide for Argentina; by LR International for Brazil; by Galileo Libros for Chile; by Ediciones ZETA S.C.R. Ltda. for Peru; by WS Computer Publishing Corporation, Inc., for the Philippines; by Contemporanea de Ediciones for Venezuela; by Express Computer Distributors for the Caribbean and West Indies; by Micronesia Media Distributor, Inc. for Micronesia; by Chips Computadoras S.A. de C.V. for Mexico; by Editorial Norma de Panama S.A. for Panama; by American Bookshops for Finland.

For general information on IDG Books Worldwide's books in the U.S., please call our Consumer Customer Service department at 800-762-2974. For reseller information, including discounts and premium sales, please call our Reseller Customer Service department at 800-434-3422.

For information on where to purchase IDG Books Worldwide's books outside the U.S., please contact our International Sales department at 317-596-5530 or fax 317-572-4002.

For consumer information on foreign language translations, please contact our Customer Service department at 1-800-434-3422, fax 317-572-4002, or e-mail rights@idgbooks.com.

For information on licensing foreign or domestic rights, please phone +1-650-653-7098.

For sales inquiries and special prices for bulk quantities, please contact our Order Services department at 800-434-3422 or write to the address above.

For information on using IDG Books Worldwide's books in the classroom or for ordering examination copies, please contact our Educational Sales department at 800-434-2086 or fax 317-572-4005.

For press review copies, author interviews, or other publicity information, please contact our Public Relations department at 650-653-7000 or fax 650-653-7500.

For authorization to photocopy items for corporate, personal, or educational use, please contact Copyright Clearance Center, 222 Rosewood Drive, Danvers, MA 01923, or fax 978-750-4470.

CLIFFSCOMPLETE

Shakespeare's

Julius Caesar

CONTENTS AT A GLANCE

CLIFFSCOMPLETE

Shakespeare's

Julius Caesar

TABLE OF CONTENTS

Shakespeare's
JULIUS CAESAR

INTRODUCTION TO WILLIAM SHAKESPEARE

William Shakespeare, or the "Bard" as people fondly call him, permeates almost all aspects of our society. He can be found in our classrooms, on our televisions, in our theatres, and in our cinemas. Speaking to us through his plays, Shakespeare comments on his life and culture, as well as our own. Actors still regularly perform his plays on the modern stage and screen. The 1990s, for example, saw the release of cinematic versions of *Romeo and Juliet, Hamlet, Othello, A Midsummer Night's Dream,* and many more of his works.

In addition to the popularity of Shakespeare's plays as he wrote them, other writers have modernized his works to attract new audiences. For example, *West Side Story* places *Romeo and Juliet* in New York City, and *A Thousand Acres* sets *King Lear* in Iowa corn country. Beyond adaptations and productions, his life and works have captured our cultural imagination. The twentieth century witnessed the production of a play about two minor characters from Shakespeare's *Hamlet* in *Rosencrantz and Guildenstern are Dead* and a fictional movie about Shakespeare's early life and poetic inspiration in *Shakespeare in Love.*

Despite his monumental presence in our culture, Shakespeare remains enigmatic. He does not tell us which plays he wrote alone, on which plays he collaborated with other playwrights, or which versions of his plays to read and perform. Furthermore, with only a handful of documents available about his life, he does not tell us much about Shakespeare the person, forcing critics and scholars to look to historical references to uncover the true-life great dramatist.

Anti-Stratfordians — modern scholars who question the authorship of Shakespeare's plays — have used this lack of information to argue that William Shakespeare either never existed or, if he did exist, did not write any of the plays we attribute to him. They believe that another historical figure, such as Francis Bacon or Queen Elizabeth I, used the name as a cover. Whether a man named William Shakespeare ever actually existed is ultimately secondary to the recognition that the group of plays bound together by that name does exist and continues to educate, enlighten, and entertain us.

An engraved portrait of Shakespeare by an unknown artist, ca. 1607.
Culver Pictures, Inc./SuperStock

Family life

Though scholars are unsure of the exact date of Shakespeare's birth, records indicate that his parents — Mary and John Shakespeare — baptized him on April 26, 1564, in the small provincial town of Stratford-upon-Avon — so named because it sat on the banks of the Avon river. Because common practice was to baptize infants a few days after they were born, scholars generally recognize April 23, 1564, as Shakespeare's birthday. Coincidentally, April 23 is the day of St. George, the patron saint of England, as well as the day upon which Shakespeare would die 52 years later. William was the third of Mary and John's eight children and the first of four sons. The house in which scholars believe Shakespeare to have been born stands on Henley Street and, despite many modifications over the years, you can still visit it today.

Shakespeare's father

Prior to Shakespeare's birth, John Shakespeare lived in Snitterfield, where he married Mary Arden, the daughter of his landlord. After moving to Stratford in 1552, he worked as a glover, a moneylender, and a dealer in agricultural products such as wool and grain. He also pursued public office and achieved a variety of posts including bailiff, Stratford's highest elected position — equivalent to a small town's mayor. At the height of his career, sometime near 1576, he petitioned the Herald's Office for a coat of arms and thus the right to be a gentleman. But the rise from the middle class to the gentry did not come right away, and the costly petition expired without being granted.

About this time, John Shakespeare mysteriously fell into financial difficulty. He became involved in serious litigation, was assessed heavy fines, and even lost his seat on the town council. Some scholars suggest that this decline could have resulted from religious discrimination because the Shakespeare family may have supported Catholicism, the practice of which was illegal in England. However, other

Shakespeare's birthplace.
SuperStock

scholars point out that not all religious dissenters (both Catholics and radical Puritans) lost their posts due to their religion. Whatever the cause of his decline, John did regain some prosperity toward the end of his life. In 1596, the Herald's Office granted the Shakespeare family a coat of arms at the petition of William, by now a successful playwright in London. And John, prior to his death in 1601, regained his seat on Stratford's town council.

Childhood and education

Our understanding of William Shakespeare's childhood in Stratford is primarily speculative because children do not often appear in the legal records from which many scholars attempt to reconstruct Shakespeare's life. Based on his father's local prominence, scholars speculate that Shakespeare most likely attended King's New School, a school that usually employed Oxford graduates and was generally well respected. Shakespeare would have started *petty school* — the rough equivalent to modern pre-school — at the age of four or five. He would have learned to read on a *hornbook*, which was a sheet of parchment or paper on which the alphabet and the Lord's Prayer were written. This sheet was framed in wood and covered with a transparent piece of horn for durability. After two years in petty school, he would have transferred to grammar school, where his school day would have probably lasted from 6 or 7 o'clock in the morning (depending on the time of year) until 5 o'clock in the evening, with only a handful of holidays.

While in grammar school, Shakespeare would primarily have studied Latin, reciting and reading the works of classical Roman authors such as Plautus, Ovid, Seneca, and Horace. Traces of these authors' works can be seen in his dramatic texts. Toward his last years in grammar school, Shakespeare would have acquired some basic skills in Greek as well. Thus the remark made by Ben Jonson, Shakespeare's well-educated friend and contemporary playwright, that Shakespeare knew "small Latin and less Greek" is accurate. Jonson is not saying that when Shakespeare left grammar school he was only semi-literate; he merely indicates that Shakespeare did not attend University, where he would have gained more Latin and Greek instruction.

Wife and children

When Shakespeare became an adult, the historical records documenting his existence began to increase. In November 1582, at the age of 18, he married 26-year-old Anne Hathaway from the nearby village of Shottery. The disparity in their ages, coupled with the fact that they baptized their first daughter, Susanna, only six months later in May 1583, has caused a great deal of modern speculation about the nature of their relationship. However, sixteenth-century conceptions of marriage differed slightly from our modern notions. Though all marriages needed to be performed before a member of the clergy, many of Shakespeare's contemporaries believed that a couple could establish a relationship through a premarital contract by exchanging vows in front of witnesses. This contract removed the social stigma of pregnancy before marriage. (Shakespeare's plays contain instances of marriage prompted by pregnancy, and *Measure for Measure* includes this kind of premarital contract.) Two years later, in February 1585, Shakespeare baptized his twins Hamnet and

Judith. Hamnet died at the age of 11 when Shakespeare was primarily living away from his family in London.

For seven years after the twins' baptism, the records remain silent on Shakespeare. At some point, he traveled to London and became involved with the theatre, but he could have been anywhere between 21 and 28 years old when he did. Though some have suggested that he may have served as an assistant to a schoolmaster at a provincial school, it seems likely that he went to London to become an actor, gradually becoming a playwright and gaining attention.

The plays: On stage and in print

The next mention of Shakespeare comes in 1592 by a University wit named Robert Greene when Shakespeare apparently was already a rising actor and playwright for the London stage. Greene, no longer a successful playwright, tried to warn other University wits about Shakespeare. He wrote:

> For there is an upstart crow, beautified with our feathers, that with his "Tiger's heart wrapped in a player's hide" supposes he is as well able to bombast out a blank verse as the best of you, and, being an absolute Johannes Factotum, is in his own conceit the only Shake-scene in a country.

This statement comes at a point in time when men without a university education, like Shakespeare, were starting to compete as dramatists with the University wits. As many critics have pointed out, Greene's statement recalls a line from *3 Henry VI*, which reads, "O tiger's heart wrapped in a woman's hide!" (I.4.137). Greene's remark does not indicate that Shakespeare was generally disliked. On the contrary, another University wit, Thomas Nashe, wrote of the great theatrical success of *Henry VI*, and Henry Chettle, Greene's publisher, later printed a flattering apology to Shakespeare. What Greene's statement does show us is that Shakespeare's reputation for poetry had reached enough of a prominence to provoke the envy of a failing competitor.

In the following year, 1593, the government closed London's theatres due to an outbreak of the bubonic plague. Publication history suggests that during this closure, Shakespeare may have written his two narrative poems, *Venus and Adonis*, published in 1593, and *The Rape of Lucrece*, published in 1594. These are the only two works that Shakespeare seems to have helped into print; each carries a dedication by Shakespeare to Henry Wriothesley, Earl of Southampton.

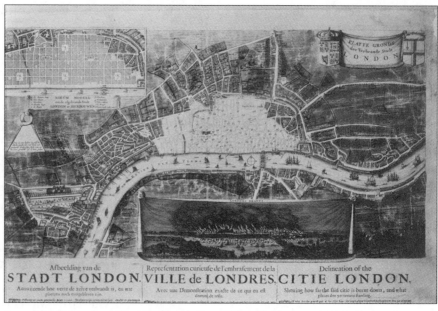

A ground plan of London after the fire of 1666, drawn by Marcus Willemsz Doornik. Guildhall Library, London/AKG, Berlin/SuperStock

Stage success

When the theatres reopened in 1594, Shakespeare joined the Lord Chamberlain's Men, an acting company. Though uncertain about the history of his early dramatic works, scholars believe that by this point he had written *The Two Gentlemen of Verona, The Taming of the Shrew,* the *Henry VI* trilogy, and *Titus Andronicus.* During his early years in the theatre, he primarily wrote history plays, with his romantic comedies emerging in the 1590s. Even at this early stage in his career, Shakespeare was a success. In 1597, he was able to purchase New Place, one of the two largest houses in Stratford, and secure a coat of arms for his family.

In 1597, the lease expired on the Lord Chamberlain's playhouse, called The Theatre. Because the owner of The Theatre refused to renew the lease, the acting company was forced to perform at various playhouses until the 1599 opening of the now famous Globe Theatre, which was literally built with lumber from The Theatre. (The Globe, later destroyed by fire, has recently been reconstructed in London and can be visited today.)

Recent scholars suggest that Shakespeare's great tragedy, *Julius Caesar*, may have been the first of Shakespeare's plays performed in the original playhouse. When this open-air theatre on the Thames River opened, financial papers list Shakespeare's name as one of the principal investors. Already an actor and a playwright, Shakespeare was now becoming a "Company Man." This new status allowed him to share in the profits of the theatre rather than merely getting paid for his plays, some of which publishers were beginning to release in quarto format.

Publications

A *quarto* was a small, inexpensive book typically used for leisure books such as plays; the term itself indicates that the printer folded the paper four times.

The modern day equivalent of a quarto would be a paperback. In contrast, the first collected works of Shakespeare were in folio format, which means that the printer folded each sheet only once. Scholars call the collected edition of Shakespeare's works the *First Folio*. A folio was a larger and more prestigious book than a quarto, and printers generally reserved the format for works such as the Bible.

No evidence exists that Shakespeare participated in the publication of any of his plays. Members of Shakespeare's acting company printed the First Folio seven years after Shakespeare's death. Generally, playwrights wrote their works to be performed on stage, and publishing them was a novel innovation at the time. Shakespeare probably would not have thought of them as books in the way we do. In fact, as a principal investor in the acting company (which purchased the play as well as the exclusive right to perform it), he may not have even thought of them as his own. He would probably have thought of his plays as belonging to the company.

For this reason, scholars have generally characterized most quartos printed before the Folio as "bad" by arguing that printers pirated the plays and published them illegally. How would a printer have received a pirated copy of a play? The theories range from someone stealing a copy to an actor (or actors) selling the play by relating it from memory to a printer. Many times, major differences exist between a quarto version of the play and a folio version, causing uncertainty about which is Shakespeare's true creation. *Hamlet*, for example, is almost twice as long in the Folio as in quarto versions. Recently, scholars have come to realize the value of the different versions. The *Norton Shakespeare*, for example, includes all three versions of *King Lear* — the quarto, the folio, and the *conflated* version (the combination of the quarto and folio).

Prolific productions

The first decade of the 1600s witnessed the publication of additional quartos as well as the production of most of Shakespeare's great tragedies, with *Julius Caesar* appearing in 1599 and *Hamlet* in 1600–1601. After the death of Queen Elizabeth in 1603, the Lord Chamberlain's Men became the King's Men under James I, Elizabeth's successor. Around the time of this transition in the English monarchy, the famous tragedy *Othello* (1603–1604) was most likely written and performed, followed closely by *King Lear* (1605–1606), *Antony and Cleopatra* (1606), and *Macbeth* (1606) in the next two years.

Shakespeare's name also appears as a major investor in the 1609 acquisition of an indoor theatre known as the Blackfriars. This last period of Shakespeare's career, which includes plays that considered the acting conditions both at the Blackfriars and the open-air Globe theatre, consists primarily of romances or tragicomedies such as *The Winter's Tale* and *The Tempest*. On June 29, 1613, during a performance of *All is True*, or *Henry VIII*, the thatching on top of The Globe caught fire and the playhouse burned to the ground. After this incident, the King's Men moved solely into the indoor Blackfriars Theatre.

Final days

During the last years of his career, Shakespeare collaborated on a couple of plays with contemporary dramatist John Fletcher, even possibly coming out of retirement — which scholars believe began sometime in 1613 — to work on *The Two Noble Kinsmen* (1613–1614). Three years later, Shakespeare died on April 23, 1616. Though the exact cause of death remains unknown, a vicar from Stratford in the mid-seventeenth-century wrote in his diary that Shakespeare, perhaps celebrating the marriage of his daughter, Judith, contracted a fever during a night of revelry with fellow literary figures Ben Jonson and Michael Drayton. Regardless, Shakespeare may have felt his death was imminent in March of that year because he altered his will. Interestingly, his will mentions no book or theatrical manuscripts, perhaps indicating the lack of value that he put on printed versions of his dramatic works and their status as company property.

Seven years after Shakespeare's death, John Heminge and Henry Condell, fellow members of the King's Men, published his collected works. In their preface, they claim that they are publishing the true versions of Shakespeare's plays partially as a response to the previous quarto printings of 18 of his plays, most of these with multiple printings. This Folio contains 36 plays to which scholars generally add *Pericles* and *The Two Noble Kinsmen*. This volume of Shakespeare's plays began the process of constructing Shakespeare not only as England's national poet but also as a monumental figure whose plays would continue to captivate imaginations at the end of the millennium with no signs of stopping. Ben Jonson's prophetic line about Shakespeare in the First Folio — "He was not of an age, but for all time!" — certainly holds true.

Chronology of Shakespeare's plays

1590–1591	*The Two Gentlemen of Verona*
	The Taming of the Shrew
1591	*2 Henry VI*
	3 Henry VI
1592	*1 Henry VI*
	Titus Andronicus
1592–1593	*Richard III*
	Venus and Adonis
1593–1594	*The Rape of Lucrece*
1594	*The Comedy of Errors*
1594–1595	*Love's Labour's Lost*
1595	*Richard II*
	Romeo and Juliet
	A Midsummer Night's Dream
1595–1596	*Love's Labour's Won*
	(This manuscript was lost.)
1596	*King John*
1596–1597	*The Merchant of Venice*
	1 Henry IV
1597–1598	*The Merry Wives of Windsor*
	2 Henry IV
1598	*Much Ado About Nothing*
1598–1599	*Henry V*
1599	*Julius Caesar*
1599–1600	*As You Like It*
1600–1601	*Hamlet*
1601	*Twelfth Night,* or *What You Will*
1602	*Troilus and Cressida*
1593–1603	*Sonnets*
1603	*Measure for Measure*
1603–1604	*A Lover's Complaint*
	Othello
1604–1605	*All's Well That Ends Well*
1605	*Timon of Athens*
1605–1606	*King Lear*
1606	*Macbeth*
	Antony and Cleopatra
1607	*Pericles*
1608	*Coriolanus*
1609	*The Winter's Tale*
1610	*Cymbeline*
1611	*The Tempest*
1612–1613	*Cardenio* (with John Fletcher;
	this manuscript was lost.)
1613	*All is True,* or *Henry VIII*
1613–1614	*The Two Noble Kinsmen*
	(with John Fletcher)

This chronology is derived from Stanley Wells' and Gary Taylor's *William Shakespeare: A Textual Companion,* which is listed in the "Works consulted" section below.

A note on Shakespeare's language

Readers encountering Shakespeare for the first time usually find Early Modern English difficult to understand. Yet, rather than serving as a barrier to Shakespeare, the richness of this language should form part of our appreciation of the Bard.

One of the first things readers usually notice about the language is the use of pronouns. Like the King James Version of the Bible, Shakespeare's pronouns are slightly different from our own and can cause confusion. Words like "thou" (you), "thee" and "ye" (objective cases of you), and "thy" and "thine" (your/yours) appear throughout Shakespeare's plays. You may need a little time to get used to these changes. You can find the definitions for other words that commonly cause confusion in the glossary column on the right side of each page in this edition.

Iambic pentameter

Though Shakespeare sometimes wrote in prose, he wrote most of his plays in poetry, specifically blank verse. Blank verse consists of lines in unrhymed *iambic pentameter. Iambic* refers to the stress patterns of the line. An *iamb* is an element of sound that consists of two beats — the first unstressed (da) and the second stressed (DA). A good example of an iambic line is Hamlet's famous line "To be or not to be," in which you do not stress "To," "or," and "to," but you do stress "be," "not," and "be." *Pentameter* refers to the *meter* or number of stressed syllables in a line. *Penta*meter has five stressed syllables. Thus, Juliet's line "But soft, what light through yonder window breaks?" (II.2.2) is a good example of an iambic pentameter line.

Wordplay

Shakespeare's language is also verbally rich as he, along with many dramatists of his period, had a fondness for wordplay. This wordplay often takes the forms of double meanings, called *puns*, where a word can mean more than one thing in a given context.

Shakespeare often employs these puns as a way of illustrating the distance between what is on the surface — *apparent* meanings — and what meanings lie underneath. Though recognizing these puns may be difficult at first, the notes in the far right column point many of them out to you.

If you are encountering Shakespeare's plays for the first time, the following reading tips may help ease you into the plays. Shakespeare's lines were meant to be spoken; therefore, reading them aloud or speaking them should help with comprehension. Also, though most of the lines are poetic, do not forget to read complete sentences — move from period to period as well as from line to line. Although Shakespeare's language can be difficult at first, the rewards of immersing yourself in the richness and fluidity of the lines are immeasurable.

Works consulted

For more information on Shakespeare's life and works, see the following:

Bevington, David, ed. *The Complete Works of Shakespeare*. New York: Longman, 1997.

Evans, G. Blakemore, ed. *The Riverside Shakespeare*. Boston: Houghton Mifflin Co., 1997.

Greenblatt, Stephen, ed. *The Norton Shakespeare*. New York: W. W. Norton and Co., 1997.

Kastan, David Scott, ed. *A Companion to Shakespeare*. Oxford: Blackwell, 1999.

McDonald, Russ. *The Bedford Companion to Shakespeare: An Introduction with Documents*. Boston: Bedford-St. Martin's Press, 1996.

Wells, Stanley and Gary Taylor. *William Shakespeare: A Textual Companion*. New York: W. W. Norton and Co., 1997.

INTRODUCTION TO EARLY MODERN ENGLAND

William Shakespeare (1564–1616) lived during a period in England's history that people have generally referred to as the English Renaissance. The term *renaissance*, meaning rebirth, was applied to this period of English history as a way of celebrating what was perceived as the rapid development of art, literature, science, and politics: in many ways, the rebirth of classical Rome.

Recently, scholars have challenged the name "English Renaissance" on two grounds. First, some scholars argue that the term should not be used because women did not share in the advancements of English culture during this time period; their legal status was still below that of men. Second, other scholars have challenged the basic notion that this period saw a sudden explosion of culture. A rebirth of civilization suggests that the previous period of time was not civilized. This second group of scholars sees a much more gradual transition between the Middle Ages and Shakespeare's time.

Some people use the terms *Elizabethan* and *Jacobean* when referring to periods of the sixteenth and seventeenth centuries. These terms correspond to the reigns of Elizabeth I (1558–1603) and James I (1603–1625). The problem with these terms is that they do not cover large spans of time; for example, Shakespeare's life and career spans both monarchies.

Scholars are now beginning to replace *Renaissance* with the term *Early Modern* when referring to this time period, but people still use both terms interchangeably. The term *Early Modern* recognizes that this period established many of the foundations of our modern culture. Though critics still disagree about the exact dates of the period, in general, the dates range from 1450 to 1750. Thus, Shakespeare's life clearly falls within the Early Modern period.

Shakespeare's plays live on in our culture, but we must remember that Shakespeare's culture differed greatly from our own. Though his understanding of human nature and relationships seems to apply to our modern lives, we must try to understand the world he lived in so we can better understand his plays. This introduction helps you do just that. It examines the intellectual, religious, political, and social contexts of Shakespeare's work before turning to the importance of the theatre and the printing press.

Intellectual context

In general, people in Early Modern England looked at the universe, the human body, and science very differently from the way we do. But while we do not share their same beliefs, we must not think of people during Shakespeare's time as lacking in intelligence or education. Discoveries made during the Early Modern period concerning the universe and the human body provide the basis of modern science.

Cosmology

One subject we view very differently than Early Modern thinkers is cosmology. Shakespeare's contemporaries believed in the astronomy of Ptolemy, an intellectual from Alexandria in the second century A.D. Ptolemy thought that the earth stood at the center of the universe, surrounded by nine concentric rings. The celestial bodies circled the earth in the following order: the moon, Mercury, Venus, the sun, Mars, Jupiter, Saturn, and the stars. The entire system was controlled by the *primum mobile*, or Prime Mover, which initiated and maintained the movement of the celestial bodies. No one had yet discovered the last three planets in our solar system, Uranus, Neptune and Pluto.

In 1543, Nicolaus Copernicus published his theory of a sun-based solar system, in which the sun stood at the center and the planets revolved around it. Though this theory appeared prior to

Shakespeare's birth, people didn't really start to change their minds until 1610, when Galileo used his telescope to confirm Copernicus' theory. David Bevington asserts in the general introduction to his edition of Shakespeare's works that during most of Shakespeare's writing career, the cosmology of the universe was in question, and this sense of uncertainty influences some of his plays.

Universal hierarchy

Closely related to Ptolemy's hierarchical view of the universe is a hierarchical conception of the Earth (sometimes referred to as the Chain of Being). During the Early Modern period, many people believed that all of creation was organized hierarchically. God existed at the top, followed by the angels, men, women, animals, plants, and rocks. (Because all women were thought to exist below all men on the chain, we can easily imagine the confusion that Elizabeth I caused when she became queen of England. She was literally "out of order," an expression that still exists in our society.) Though the concept of this hierarchy is a useful one when beginning to study Shakespeare, keep in mind that distinctions in this hierarchical view were not always clear and that we should not reduce all Early Modern thinking to a simple chain.

Elements and humors

The belief in a hierarchical scheme of existence created a comforting sense of order and balance that carried over into science as well. Shakespeare's contemporaries generally accepted that four different elements composed everything in the universe: earth, air, water, and fire. People associated these four elements with four qualities of being. These qualities — hot, cold, moist, and dry — appeared in different combinations in the elements. For example, air was hot and moist; water was cold and moist; earth was cold and dry; and fire was hot and dry.

In addition, people believed that the human body contained all four elements in the form of *humors* — blood, phlegm, yellow bile, and black bile — each of which corresponded to an element. Blood corresponded to air (hot and moist), phlegm to water (cold and moist), yellow bile to fire (hot and dry), and black bile to earth (cold and dry). When someone was sick, physicians generally believed that the patient's humors were not in the proper balance. For example, if someone were diagnosed with an abundance of blood, the physician would bleed the patient (using leeches or cutting the skin) in order to restore the balance.

Shakespeare's contemporaries also believed that the humors determined personality and temperament. If a person's dominant humor was blood, he was considered lighthearted. If dominated by yellow bile (or choler), that person was irritable. The dominance of phlegm led a person to be dull and kind. And if black bile prevailed, he was melancholy or sad. Thus, people of Early Modern England often used the humors to explain behavior and emotional outbursts. Throughout Shakespeare's plays, he uses the concept of the humors to define and explain various characters. In the play *Julius Caesar*, the humors are referred to on several occasions. For example, in Act IV, Scene 3, the famous "quarrel scene," Brutus accuses a testy Cassius of having a "rash choler."

Religious context

Shakespeare lived in an England full of religious uncertainty and dispute. From the Protestant Reformation to the translation of the Bible into English, the Early Modern era is punctuated with events that have greatly influenced modern religious beliefs.

The Reformation

Until the Protestant Reformation, the only Christian church was the Catholic, or "universal," church.

Beginning in Europe in the early sixteenth century, religious thinkers such as Martin Luther and John Calvin, who claimed that the Roman Catholic Church had become corrupt and was no longer following the word of God, began what has become known as the Protestant Reformation. The Protestants ("protestors") believed in salvation by faith rather than works. They also believed in the primacy of the Bible and advocated giving all people access to reading the Bible.

A portrait of King Henry VIII, artist unknown, ca. 1542.
National Portrait Gallery, London/SuperStock

Many English people initially resisted Protestant ideas. However, the Reformation in England began in 1527 during the reign of Henry VIII, prior to Shakespeare's birth. In that year, Henry VIII decided to divorce his wife, Catherine of Aragon, for her failure to produce a male heir. (Only one of their children, Mary, survived past infancy.) Rome denied Henry's petitions for a divorce, forcing him to divorce Catherine without the Church's approval, which he did in 1533.

The Act of Supremacy

The following year, the Pope excommunicated Henry VIII while Parliament confirmed his divorce and the legitimacy of his new marriage through the *Act of Succession*. Later in 1534, Parliament passed the *Act of Supremacy*, naming Henry the "Supreme Head of the Church in England." Henry continued to persecute both radical Protestant reformers and Catholics who remained loyal to Rome.

Henry VIII's death in 1547 brought Edward VI, his 10-year-old son by Jane Seymour (the king's third wife), to the throne. This succession gave Protestant reformers the chance to solidify their break with the Catholic Church. During Edward's reign, Archbishop Thomas Cranmer established the foundation for the Anglican Church through his 42 articles of religion. He also wrote the first *Book of Common Prayer*, adopted in 1549, which was the official text for worship services in England.

Bloody Mary

Catholics continued to be persecuted until 1553, when the sickly Edward VI died and was succeeded by Mary, his half-sister and the Catholic daughter of Catherine of Aragon. The reign of Mary witnessed the reversal of religion in England through the restoration of Catholic authority and obedience to Rome. Protestants were executed in large numbers, which earned the monarch the nickname "Bloody Mary." Many Protestants fled to Europe to escape persecution.

Elizabeth, the daughter of Henry VIII and Anne Boleyn, outwardly complied with the mandated Catholicism during her half-sister Mary's reign, but she restored Protestantism when she took the throne in 1558 after Mary's death. Thus, in the space of a single decade, England's throne passed from Protestant to Catholic to Protestant, with each change carrying serious and deadly consequences.

Though Elizabeth reigned in relative peace from 1558 until her death in 1603, religion was still a serious concern for her subjects. During Shakespeare's life, a great deal of religious dissent existed in England. Many Catholics, who remained loyal to Rome and their church, were persecuted for their beliefs. At the other end of the spectrum, the Puritans were persecuted for their belief that the Reformation was not complete. (The English pejoratively applied the term *Puritan* to religious groups that wanted to continue purifying the English church by such measures as removing the *episcopacy,* or the structure of bishops.)

The Great Bible

One thing agreed upon by both the Anglicans and Puritans was the importance of a Bible written in English. Translated by William Tyndale in 1525, the first authorized Bible in English, published in 1539, was known as the Great Bible. This Bible was later revised during Elizabeth's reign into what was known as the Bishop's Bible. As Stephen Greenblatt points out in his introduction to the *Norton Shakespeare,* Shakespeare would probably have been familiar with both the Bishop's Bible, heard aloud in Mass, and the Geneva Bible, which was written by English exiles in Geneva. The last authorized Bible produced during Shakespeare's lifetime came within the last decade of his life when James I's commissioned edition, known as the King James Bible, appeared in 1611.

Political context

Politics and religion were closely related in Shakespeare's England. Both of the monarchs under whom Shakespeare lived had to deal with religious and political dissenters.

Elizabeth I

Despite being a Protestant, Elizabeth I tried to take a middle road on the religious question. She allowed Catholics to practice their religion in private as long as they outwardly appeared Anglican and remained loyal to the throne.

Elizabeth's monarchy was one of absolute supremacy. Believing in the divine right of kings, she styled herself as being appointed by God to rule England. To oppose the Queen's will was the equivalent of opposing God's will. Known as *passive obedience,* this doctrine did not allow any opposition even to a tyrannical monarch because God had appointed the king or queen for reasons unknown to His subjects on earth. However, as Bevington notes, Elizabeth's power was not as absolute as her rhetoric suggested. Parliament, already well established in England, reserved some power, such as the authority to levy taxes, for itself.

A portrait of Elizabeth I by George Gower, ca. 1588. National Portrait Gallery, London/SuperStock

Elizabeth I lived in a society that restricted women from possessing any political or personal autonomy and power. As queen, Elizabeth violated and called into question many of the prejudices and practices against women. In a way, her society forced her to "overcome" her sex in order to rule effectively. However, her position did nothing to increase the status of women in England.

One of the rhetorical strategies that Elizabeth adopted in order to rule effectively was to separate her position as monarch of England from her natural body — to separate her *body politic* from her *body natural*. In addition, throughout her reign, Elizabeth brilliantly negotiated between domestic and foreign factions — some of whom were anxious about a female monarch and wanted her to marry — appeasing both sides without ever committing to one.

She remained unmarried throughout her 45-year reign, partially by styling herself as the Virgin Queen whose purity represented England herself. Her refusal to marry and her habit of hinting and promising marriage with suitors both foreign and domestic helped Elizabeth maintain internal and external peace. Not marrying allowed her to retain her independence, but it left the succession of the English throne in question. In 1603, on her deathbed, she named James VI, King of Scotland and son of her cousin Mary, as her successor.

James I

When he assumed the English crown, James VI of Scotland became James I of England. (Some historians refer to him as James VI and I.) Like Elizabeth, James was a strong believer in the divine right of kings and their absolute authority.

Upon his arrival in London to claim the English throne, James made his plans to unite Scotland and England clear. However, a long-standing history of enmity existed between the two countries. Partially as a result of this history and the influx of Scottish

courtiers into English society, anti-Scottish prejudice abounded in England. When James asked Parliament for the title of "King of Great Britain," he was denied.

As scholars such as Bevington have pointed out, James was less successful than Elizabeth was in negotiating between the different religious and political factions in England. Although he was a Protestant, he began to have problems with the Puritan sect of the House of Commons, which ultimately led to a rift between the court (which also started to have Catholic sympathies) and the Parliament. This rift between the monarchy and Parliament eventually escalated into the civil war that would erupt during the reign of James's son, Charles I.

In spite of its difficulties with Parliament, James' court was a site of wealth, luxury, and extravagance. James I commissioned elaborate feasts, masques, and pageants, and in doing so he more than doubled the royal debt. Stephen Greenblatt suggests that Shakespeare's *The Tempest* may reflect this extravagance through Prospero's magnificent banquet and accompanying masque. Reigning from 1603 to 1625, James I remained the King of England throughout the last years of Shakespeare's life.

Social context

Shakespeare's England divided itself roughly into two social classes: the aristocrats (or nobility) and everyone else. The primary distinctions between these two classes were ancestry, wealth, and power. Simply put, the aristocrats were the only ones who possessed all three.

Aristocrats were born with their wealth, but the growth of trade and the development of skilled professions began to provide wealth for those not born with it. Although the notion of a middle class did not begin to develop until after Shakespeare's death, the possibility of some social mobility did exist in

Early Modern England. Shakespeare himself used the wealth gained from the theatre to move into the lower ranks of the aristocracy by securing a coat of arms for his family.

Shakespeare was not unique in this movement, but not all people received the opportunity to increase their social status. Members of the aristocracy feared this social movement and, as a result, promoted harsh laws of apprenticeship and fashion, restricting certain styles of dress and material. These laws dictated that only the aristocracy could wear certain articles of clothing, colors, and materials. Though enforcement was a difficult task, the Early Modern aristocracy considered dressing above one's station a moral and ethical violation.

The status of women

The legal status of women did not allow them much public or private autonomy. English society functioned on a system of patriarchy and hierarchy (see "Universal hierarchy" earlier in this introduction), which means that men controlled society beginning with the individual family. In fact, the family metaphorically corresponded to the state. For example, the husband was the king of his family. His authority to control his family was absolute and based on divine right, similar to that of the country's king. People also saw the family itself differently than today, considering apprentices and servants part of the whole family.

The practice of *primogeniture* — a system of inheritance that passed all of a family's wealth through the first male child — accompanied this system of patriarchy. Thus women did not generally inherit their family's wealth and titles. In the absence of a male heir, some women, such as Queen Elizabeth, did. But after women married, they lost almost all of their already limited legal rights, such as the right to inherit, to own property, and to sign contracts. In all likelihood, Elizabeth I would have lost much of her power and authority if she married.

Furthermore, women did not generally receive an education and could not enter certain professions, including acting. Instead, society relegated women to the domestic sphere of the home.

Although there are only two women in *Julius Caesar*, Brutus' wife, Portia, gives the reader an interesting look at Roman women through Elizabethan eyes. In Act II, Scene 1, Portia is concerned about her husband's recent erratic behavior. Instead of remaining the silent, complacent wife, Portia confronts her husband, asking Brutus to treat her as a respected equal by revealing his secrets to her. She reminds him that she is an honorable and constant woman, strong enough to bear anything her husband may reveal to her. Brutus eventually tells Portia his plans, but by Act II, Scene 4, under the burdens of those secrets, Portia laments, "how weak a thing / The heart of woman is." Frantic that she will betray her husband, Portia complains that she has "a man's mind, but a woman's might. / How hard it is for women to keep counsel."

Daily life

Daily life in Early Modern England began before sun-up — exactly how early depended on one's station in life. A servant's responsibilities usually included preparing the house for the day. Families usually possessed limited living space, and even among wealthy families multiple family members tended to share a small number of rooms, suggesting that privacy may not have been important or practical.

Working through the morning, Elizabethans usually had lunch about noon. This midday meal was the primary meal of the day, much like dinner is for modern families. The workday usually ended around sundown or 5:00 p.m., depending on the season. Before an early bedtime, Elizabethans usually ate a light repast and then settled in for a couple of hours of reading (if the family members were literate and could bear the high cost of books) or socializing.

Mortality rates

Mortality rates in Early Modern England were high compared to our standards, especially among infants. Infection and disease ran rampant because physicians did not realize the need for antiseptics and sterile equipment. As a result, communicable diseases often spread very rapidly in cities, particularly London.

In addition, the bubonic plague frequently ravaged England, with two major outbreaks — from 1592–1594 and in 1603 — occurring during Shakespeare's lifetime. People did not understand the plague and generally perceived it as God's punishment. (We now know that the plague was spread by fleas and could not be spread directly from human to human.) Without a cure or an understanding of what transmitted the disease, physicians could do nothing to stop the thousands of deaths that resulted from each outbreak. These outbreaks had a direct effect on Shakespeare's career, because the government often closed the theatres in an effort to impede the spread of the disease.

London life

In the sixteenth century, London, though small compared to modern cities, was the largest city of Europe, with a population of about 200,000 inhabitants in the city and surrounding suburbs. London was a crowded city without a sewer system, which facilitated epidemics such as the plague. In addition, crime rates were high in the city due to inefficient law enforcement and the lack of street lighting.

Despite these drawbacks, London was the cultural, political, and social heart of England. As the home of the monarch and most of England's trade, London was a bustling metropolis. Not surprisingly, a young Shakespeare moved to London to begin his professional career.

The theatre

Most theatres were not actually located within the city of London. Rather, theatre owners built them on the South bank of the Thames River (in Southwark) across from the city in order to avoid the strict regulations that applied within the city's walls. These restrictions stemmed from a mistrust of public performances as locations of plague and riotous behavior. Furthermore, because theatre performances took place during the day, they took laborers away from their jobs. Opposition to the theatres also came from Puritans who believed that they fostered immorality. Therefore, theatres moved out of the city, to areas near other sites of restricted activities, such as dog fighting, bear- and bull-baiting, and prostitution.

Despite the move, the theatre was not free from censorship or regulation. In fact, a branch of the government known as the Office of the Revels attempted to ensure that plays did not present politically or socially sensitive material. Prior to each performance, the Master of the Revels would read a complete text of each play, cutting out offending sections or, in some cases, not approving the play for public performance.

The recently reconstructed Globe Theatre.
Chris Parker/PAL

Performance spaces

Theatres in Early Modern England were quite different from our modern facilities. They were usually open-air, relying heavily on natural light and good weather. The rectangular stage extended out into an area that people called the *pit* — a circular, uncovered area about 70 feet in diameter. Audience members had two choices when purchasing admission to a theatre. Admission to the pit, where the lower classes (or *groundlings*) stood for the performances, was the cheaper option. People of wealth could purchase a seat in one of the three covered tiers of seats that ringed the pit. At full capacity, a public theatre in Early Modern England could hold between 2,000 and 3,000 people.

The stage, which projected into the pit and was raised about five feet above it, had a covered portion called the *heavens*. The heavens enclosed theatrical equipment for lowering and raising actors to and from the stage. A trapdoor in the middle of the stage provided theatrical graves for characters such as Ophelia and also allowed ghosts, such as Banquo in *Macbeth*, to rise from the earth. A wall separated the back of the stage from the actors' dressing room, known as the *tiring house*. At each end of the wall stood a door for major entrances and exits. Above the wall and doors stood a gallery directly above the stage, reserved for the wealthiest spectators. Actors occasionally used this area when a performance called for a difference in height — for example, to represent Juliet's balcony or the walls of a besieged city. A good example of this type of theatre was the original

Shakespeare in Love *shows how the interior of the Globe would have appeared.*
Everett Collection

Globe Theatre in London in which Shakespeare's company, The Lord Chamberlain's Men (later the King's Men), staged its plays. However, indoor theatres, such as the Blackfriars, differed slightly because the pit was filled with chairs that faced a rectangular stage. Because only the wealthy could afford the cost of admission, the public generally considered these theatres private.

The Globe Theatre was partially owned by William Shakespeare and was an example of the type of outdoor theatre described above. When Cuthbert Burbage, another partner in Shakespeare's acting company, The Chamberlain's Men, was unable to renew the ground lease for the theatre they used before 1599, he had the old theatre dismantled and rebuilt in Southwark, just outside London. The newly rebuilt Globe opened to audiences in the middle of 1599 and some scholars believe that *Julius Caesar* was the first play to be performed in the new theatre.

Actors and staging

Performances in Shakespeare's England do not appear to have employed scenery. However, theatre companies developed their costumes with great care and expense. In fact, a playing company's costumes were its most valuable items. These extravagant costumes were the object of much controversy because some aristocrats feared that the actors could use them to disguise their social status on the streets of London.

Costumes also disguised a player's gender. All actors on the stage during Shakespeare's lifetime were men. Young boys whose voices had not reached maturity played female parts. This practice no doubt influenced Shakespeare's and his contemporary playwrights' thematic explorations of cross-dressing.

Though historians have managed to reconstruct the appearance of the early modern theatre, such as the recent construction of the Globe in London, much of the information regarding how plays were performed during this era has been lost. Scholars of Early Modern theatre have turned to the scant external and internal stage directions in manuscripts in an effort to find these answers. Although a hindrance for modern critics and scholars, the lack of detail about Early Modern performances has allowed modern directors and actors a great deal of flexibility and room to be creative.

The printing press

If not for the printing press, many Early Modern plays may not have survived until today. In Shakespeare's time, printers produced all books by *sheet* — a single large piece of paper that the printer would fold in order to produce the desired book size. For example, a folio required folding the sheet once, a quarto four times, an octavo eight, and so on. Sheets would be printed one side at a time; thus, printers had to simultaneously print multiple nonconsecutive pages.

In order to estimate what section of the text would be on each page, the printer would *cast off* copy. After the printer made these estimates, *compositors* would set the type upside down, letter by letter. This process of setting type produced textual errors, some of which a proofreader would catch. When a proofreader found an error, the compositors would fix the piece or pieces of type. Printers called corrections made after printing began *stop-press* corrections because they literally had to stop the press to fix the error. Because of the high cost of paper, printers would still sell the sheets printed before they made the correction.

Printers placed frames of text in the bed of the printing press and used them to imprint the paper. They then folded and grouped the sheets of paper into gatherings, after which the pages were ready for sale. The buyer had the option of getting the new play bound.

The printing process was crucial to the preservation of Shakespeare's works, but the printing of drama in Early Modern England was not a standardized practice. Many of the first editions of Shakespeare's plays appear in quarto format and, until recently, scholars regarded them as "corrupt." In fact, scholars still debate how close a relationship exists between what appeared on the stage in the sixteenth and seventeenth centuries and what appears on the printed page. The inconsistent and scant appearance of stage directions, for example, makes it difficult to determine how close this relationship was.

We know that the practice of the theatre allowed the alteration of plays by a variety of hands other than the author's, further complicating any efforts to extract what a playwright wrote and what was changed by either the players, the printers, or the government censors. Theatre was a collaborative environment. Rather than lament our inability to determine authorship and what exactly Shakespeare wrote, we should work to understand this collaborative nature and learn from it.

The text of *Julius Caesar* exists in only one form as it was printed in the 1623 Folio collection of the plays. Based on the number of stage directions included in the script, the compositors were most likely working from a theatrical prompt book or a copy of that document.

Shakespeare wrote his plays for the stage, and the existing published texts reflect the collaborative nature of the theatre as well as the unavoidable changes made during the printing process. A play's first written version would have been the author's *foul papers*, which invariably consisted of blotted lines and revised text. From there, a scribe would recopy the play and produce a *fair copy*. The theatre manager would then copy out and annotate this copy into a playbook (what people today call a *prompt-book*).

At this point, scrolls of individual parts were copied out for actors to memorize. (Due to the high cost of paper, theatre companies could not afford to provide their actors with a complete copy of the play.) The government required the company to send the playbook to the Master of the Revels, the government official who would make any necessary changes or mark any passages considered unacceptable for performance.

Printers could have used any one of these copies to print a play. We cannot determine whether a printer used the author's version, the modified theatrical version, the censored version, or a combination when printing a given play. Refer back to the "Publications" section of the "Introduction to William Shakespeare" for further discussion of the impact printing practices has on our understanding of Shakespeare's works.

Works cited

For more information regarding Early Modern England, consult the following works:

Bevington, David. "General Introduction." *The Complete Works of William Shakespeare*. Updated Fourth edition. New York: Longman, 1997.

Greenblatt, Stephen. "Shakespeare's World." *Norton Shakespeare*. New York: W. W. Norton and Co., 1997.

Kastan, David Scott, ed. *A Companion to Shakespeare*. Oxford: Blackwell, 1999.

McDonald, Russ. *The Bedford Companion to Shakespeare: An Introduction with Documents*. Boston: Bedford-St. Martin's Press, 1996.

INTRODUCTION TO JULIUS CAESAR

The seemingly straightforward simplicity of *Julius Caesar* has made it a perennial favorite for almost 400 years. Despite its simplicity, almost Roman in nature, the play is rich both dramatically and thematically, and every generation since Shakespeare's time has been able to identify with some political aspect of the play. The Victorians found a stoic, sympathetic character in Brutus and found Caesar unforgivably weak and tyrannical. As we move into the twenty-first century, audiences and readers, familiar with leaders having public imperfections, are more forgiving of Caesar and are often suspicious of Brutus' moralistic posturing. The play has also formed most modern readers' opinions and views of ancient Rome and Romans. In the article, "Shakespeare and the Elizabethan Romans," published in *Shakespeare Survey* #10 in 1957, critic T.J.B. Spencer wrote, "The part played by Shakespeare himself in creating our notions of the ancient Romans should not be forgotten . . . we are all in the power of Shakespeare's imagination, a power which has been exercised for several generations and from which it is scarcely possible to extricate ourselves."

The structure of the play follows closely the pattern of the typical Elizabethan revenge play but varies in form from Shakespeare's other history plays.

Revenge plays, extremely popular in the theatre of Shakespeare's day, dealt with the retribution of an evil act. For example, a murder was always punished by another murder and often under the auspices of the original victim's ghost. The person who committed the first murder, regardless of personal honor or motives, was doomed from the beginning. *Julius Caesar*, a play that deals with actual historical events, differs somewhat from the plays that Shakespeare wrote about English history. As Judah Stampfer points out in *The Tragic Engagement: A Study of Shakespeare's Classical Tragedies*, Shakespeare's English history plays sought to establish some sort of legitimacy by the end of the play. But *Julius Caesar* consists of one illegitimate act after another. Caesar overthrows Pompey and damages the republic. Brutus and the other conspirators plot to assassinate Caesar, mob rule is tolerated, Antony instructs Octavius in Machiavellian ethics and the play ends with Octavius positioning for authority, with civil war imminent.

The majority of Shakespeare's plays are written in blank verse and *Julius Caesar* is no exception. Blank verse is a form of poetry in iambic pentameter. Each line has ten syllables — five unstressed syllables alternating with five stressed syllables. Occasionally, a word that is usually pronounced as one syllable is accompanied by a grave accent. The accent is an indication that the word should be spoken with two syllables. For example, the word "moved," usually one syllable, with a grave accent would be pronounced as "move-ed." This allows the line to fall correctly into the rhythm of the iambic pentameter.

During the Renaissance, there was a rekindling of interest in ancient Roman literature and art. Thus, the subject matter was of great interest to Elizabethan audiences. Shakespeare wrote a total of four plays set in ancient Rome. In addition to *Julius Caesar*, Shakespeare's Roman plays include *Titus Andronicus*, *Antony and Cleopatra*, and *Coriolanus*. Shakespeare was especially interested in the character of Julius Caesar and mentions him consistently in his other plays, including *Hamlet, Richard III, As You Like It, Henry IV, Parts 1 and 2*, and *Henry VI, Parts 2 and 3*.

Date and text

Julius Caesar is speculated to be Shakespeare's twenty-first play, written at the end of the cycle of history plays and just before *Hamlet*. The play was first performed, and thus, thought to have been written, in 1599 and may have been the premier show of the newly rebuilt Globe Theatre. This date is based on the journal of a Swiss traveler, Thomas Platter, who was visiting England between September 18 and October 20, 1599, and attended two plays. In his journal, translated by Ernest Schanzer in the article, "Thomas Platter's Observations on the Elizabethan Stage," published in *Notes & Queries* in 1956, Platter described one of the plays that he saw and many scholars believe he is writing about Shakespeare's play, *Julius Caesar*, being performed at The Globe:

> After lunch on September 21st, at about two o'clock, I and my party crossed the river, and there in the house with the thatched roof we saw an excellent performance of the tragedy of the first Emperor Julius Caesar with about fifteen characters; after the play, according to their custom they did a most elegant and curious dance, two dressed in men's clothes, and two in women's.

Not published during Shakespeare's lifetime, *Julius Caesar* appeared for the first time seven years after his death in the First Folio of 1623. The play appeared in the Folio as *The Tragedy of Julius Caesar* but was listed as *The Life and Death of Julius Caesar* in the table of contents. The text of *Julius Caesar*, as it appears in the Folio, is relatively error-free and has the reputation of being the least corrupt text printed in the Folio. Because the play is so rich in stage directions, it is thought that the compositors of the 1623 Folio were most likely working from a prompt book or a transcript of that document. A prompt book is a copy of the text used by the stage manager of a theatre. It is marked with character entrances and exits, blocking, props, and special effects such as offstage shouts, music, or sounds of thunder and lightening.

Shakespeare's sources

The majority of Shakespeare's information about the people and events in *Julius Caesar* was taken from the work of the Greek historian, Plutarch (46?–120? A.D.). Sir Thomas North, working from the French version of Plutarch's works translated by Jacques Amyot, published an English language version of Plutarch's *Lives of the Noble Grecians and Romans* in 1579. It was reprinted in 1595 with minimal changes and again in 1603 with the addition of the life of Octavius Caesar. Working from North's translations, Shakespeare used material from the *Lives* of Julius Caesar, Marcus Antonius, and Marcus Brutus.

Because Plutarch was as interested in the moral characteristics of his subjects as he was in the historical facts, Shakespeare found very useful information in the stories that would translate well onto the theatrical stage. Plutarch's telling of the lives of Caesar, Antony, and Brutus is rich with anecdotes about the characters as well as descriptions of appearance and personality traits. Being the consummate playwright, however, Shakespeare was able to embellish the stories adding compressed action, heightened drama, and powerful speeches as well as internal and external conflict.

Many speeches from the play are taken directly from North's translation and are only rephrased to fit into blank verse. For example, in the *Life of Brutus,* Plutarch records Brutus as saying, "It rejoiceth my heart, that not one of my friends hath failed me at my need." Shakespeare has Brutus say, "My heart doth joy that yet in all my life / I found no man but

was true to me" (V.5.34–35). The Forum speeches, as delivered by Brutus and Antony, are results of Shakespeare's imagination and proof of his enduring genius.

Other sources that Shakespeare may have used for *Julius Caesar* include a biography of Julius Caesar by John Higgins in *A Mirror for Magistrates* and Chaucer's "The Monk's Tale" from *The Canterbury Tales,* in which Brutus and Cassius are seen as spiteful assassins and Caesar becomes an honorable sacrifice. Shakespeare my also have been influenced by Dante's *Divine Comedy*, in which Brutus and Cassius are seen in the lowest circle of hell alongside Judas Iscariot.

Performance history

The first performance of *Julius Caesar* occurred in 1599. According to the Swiss traveler, Thomas Platter, the play was "very well acted" and "elaborately costumed." Although most costuming in Elizabethan theatres was minimal, it is conjectured that there was some classical costuming in the production of *Julius Caesar* including the use of breastplates and plumed helmets. The play was extremely popular with the original audience and Leonard Digges wrote about the enthusiastic audiences for the play as late as the 1620s. There is proof that the play was performed at Whitehall in 1611 and 1612, at Saint James in January of 1636 and at the Cock Pit in the same year. The play was performed for Charles I in 1637 and remained an audience favorite right up to 1642 when the theatres were closed because of the English Civil War.

When Charles II was restored to the throne in 1660, the theatres were reopened. *Julius Caesar* was included in the repertoire of Thomas Kilgrew's Company in the 1660s and was one of the few plays written by Shakespeare that remained popular in the late seventeenth century. With many changes to the script and alterations to the major characters, *Julius Caesar* continued to draw audiences into the theatre.

A 1953 film poster potraying the assassination of Julius Caesar.
Everett Collection

From 1708 to 1728 the character of Brutus took center stage in productions of the play. Famous actors of the time, such as Thomas Betterton, Barton Booth, and James Quin all took their turns playing the character that was being performed as the stoical and dignified hero of the play. The text was often altered so that Caesar became a frightening tyrant and the character of Antony was restructured to be a freedom fighter, played by such luminaries as Edward Kynaston, Robert Wilks, and William Milward. The play was often cut and rearranged to make the focus of the play a battle between good and evil or ambition and liberty. Fearing the audience's reaction to the violence, the scene with Cinna the poet was cut so as not to offend the audience; Portia's gash was moved from her thigh to her arm for the same reason. During the years of 1750–1780, *Julius Caesar* was revived almost every year with 150 performances in London.

The play, appealing to the ideals of the early American settlers, was first performed in America on June 1, 1770, in Philadelphia. An advertisement for the play read: "The noble struggles for liberty by that renowned patriot, Marcus Brutus." America's connection to *Julius Caesar* took an interesting turn during the American Civil War. President Abraham Lincoln was assassinated by a member of one of the most famous acting families of the time, John Wilkes Booth. Booth's father, Junius Brutus Booth, was named after the Brutus who had murdered Julius Caesar. Both John Wilkes and his father Junius Brutus performed in a benefit performance of *Julius Caesar*, staged to raise money to erect a statue of William Shakespeare in New York's Central Park on November 25, 1864. Four months later, during a performance of *Our American Cousin*, John Wilkes Booth shot and killed President Lincoln. Booth jumped from the president's box to the stage shouting the motto of the state of Virginia, "Sic Semper Tyrannis" (Thus Be It Ever To Tyrants).

Great scenic spectacles that prided themselves on realistic sets, lavish costumes, and huge crowds of people on stage (as opposed to focusing on the content of the script being performed) dominated the theatre in the early nineteenth century. John Phillip Kemble, working at the Theatre Royal and Covent Garden, turned *Julius Caesar* into a sensational event that was visually stunning but again altered Shakespeare's script to fit the mores and ideals of the time.

Brutus remained a lofty patriot and the scene in which Antony and Octavius mark people for death was cut. Herbert Beerbohm Tree, managing Her Majesty's Theatre in 1898, cut both scenes and characters to make Antony the star of the play and his production became the defining production of *Julius Caesar* for the next twenty years. W. C. Macready, who played at one time or another both Brutus and Cassius, maintained the grandiose style of Kemble and Tree but, seeing the richness of the characters as drawn by Shakespeare, began to play the men as written with both their positive and negative qualities. He also made the assassination scene realistic and bloody and set the stage for the reinstatement of the "original" text in the twentieth century.

In Act III, Scene 1, of *Julius Caesar*, Shakespeare has Cassius ask, "How many ages hence / Shall this our lofty scene be acted over / In states unborn and accents yet unknown!" Reviewing the twentieth century productions of *Julius Caesar*, one might be tempted to add prophet to Shakespeare's list of accomplishments. With the majority of the text restored to Shakespeare's script, the themes and character conflicts begin to take precedence over the visual presentation. Modern producers and directors became aware of the contemporary nature of the themes in *Julius Caesar* and productions of the twentieth century reflected that discovery. On the modern stage, Caesar has become versions of Hitler, Mussolini, and Fidel Castro. In a production at the Barons Court Theatre in 1993, a woman played Caesar as a character reminiscent of former British Prime Minister Margaret Thatcher. The crowds have at times become Nazi rallies and audiences have actually been encouraged to participate as members of the mob in several productions. Caesar's influence after his death has been represented with huge statues left on stage to tower over the action and, in 1957, Glenn Byam Shaw, in his production at the Royal Shakespeare Theatre in Stratford, England, projected a star that was prominent during the funeral scene and again over the plains of Philippi. *Julius Caesar*, along with all of Shakespeare's plays, with their universal themes and uncanny understanding of human nature, will continue to find a place on the stage and in the hearts of audiences everywhere.

Criticism

The first critics, writing at the end of the seventeenth century, were not kind to *Julius Caesar*. Critics such as Thomas Rymer and John Dennis expressed their dissatisfaction with the minor role that Caesar had

A modern stage production of Julius Caesar.
Clive Barda/PAL

in a play that bore his name and with what they felt were historical inaccuracies. Writing in 1817, William Hazlitt, in his book, *Characters of Shakespeares Plays*, disapproved of the fact that Caesar, as drawn by Shakespeare, was not like "the portrait given of him in his commentaries."

In addition to what many felt was the disregard of the unity of time, place, and action, the major complaint in much of the early criticism of the play lay with the hero. If Julius Caesar, as written by Shakespeare, was the hero of the play, he was, at best, a deficient hero. Charles Gildon in his preface to *Julius Caesar* in Nicholas Rowe's 1710 edition of Shakespeare's works, claimed that the true hero of the piece was Brutus and that opinion held for almost 200 years. Samuel Johnson exonerated the play in his Preface of 1765 and Herman Ulrici, writing in 1839, found a thematic unity to the play never acknowledged before. This led to a renewed interest in the play by critics in the nineteenth century.

In the early twentieth century, critics such as M.W. MacCallum began studying the play as it referred to Plutarch, finding a new historical interest in Shakespeare's source material. G. Wilson Knight, writing in the 1930s, discovered much of interest in Shakespeare's use of language and imagery; the characters of Caesar and Brutus were appreciated for their human ambiguities during this time period by such critics as Dover Wilson. Character study gave way to the examination of the play's moral and political themes, and critics such as Harley Granville-Barker in 1947 and R.A. Foakes in 1954 found the play's unity in its political themes. In the latter part of the twentieth century, the play and its political overtones underwent scrutiny by both the New Historicists and the Cultural Materialists. Coppelia Kahn in her 1997 book, *Roman Shakespeare: Warriors, Wounds and Women*, gives a very interesting look at the Roman plays, including *Julius Caesar*,

from a feminist perspective. As Shakespearean criticism moves into the twenty-first century, there seems to be a movement towards reexamining Shakespeare in the context in which it was written. As David Scott Kastan writes in *Shakespeare After Theory* (1999), the movement is to:

> ...*restore Shakespeare's artistry to the earliest conditions of its realization and intelligibility: to the collaborations of the theater in which the plays were acted, to the practices of the book trade in which they were published, to the unstable political world of late Tudor and early Stuart England in which the plays were engaged by their various publics.*

CHARACTERS IN THE PLAY

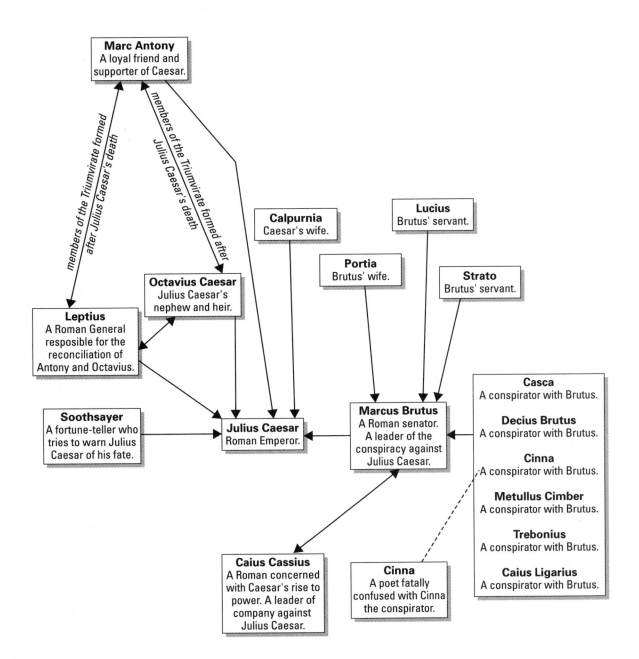

Marc Antony
A loyal friend and supporter of Caesar.

members of the Triumvirate formed after Julius Caesar's death

members of the Triumvirate formed after Julius Caesar's death

Calpurnia
Caesar's wife.

Lucius
Brutus' servant.

Portia
Brutus' wife.

Strato
Brutus' servant.

Octavius Caesar
Julius Caesar's nephew and heir.

Leptius
A Roman General resposible for the reconciliation of Antony and Octavius.

Soothsayer
A fortune-teller who tries to warn Julius Caesar of his fate.

Julius Caesar
Roman Emperor.

Marcus Brutus
A Roman senator. A leader of the conspiracy against Julius Caesar.

Casca
A conspirator with Brutus.

Decius Brutus
A conspirator with Brutus.

Cinna
A conspirator with Brutus.

Metullus Cimber
A conspirator with Brutus.

Trebonius
A conspirator with Brutus.

Caius Ligarius
A conspirator with Brutus.

Caius Cassius
A Roman concerned with Caesar's rise to power. A leader of company against Julius Caesar.

Cinna
A poet fatally confused with Cinna the conspirator.

JULIUS CAESAR
ACT I

Cassuis *Fellow, come from the throng; look upon Caesar.*

Caesar *What say 'st thou to me now? Speak once again.*

Soothsayer *Beware the ides of March.*

Caesar *He is a dreamer. Let us leave him. Pass.*

Act I, Scene 1

A rowdy group of plebians or commoners have gathered in the streets of Rome to celebrate both the Feast of the Lupercal and Julius Caesar's triumphant return to Rome after defeating the last of his enemies, the sons of Pompey. Two tribunes, Marullus and Flavius, chastise the crowd for adoring Caesar and for celebrating as if it were a holiday. The crowd guiltily disperses and Marullus and Flavius depart to vandalize Caesar's statues.

ACT I, SCENE 1.
Rome, a street.

[*Enter* FLAVIUS, MARULLUS, *and certain commoners over the stage.*]

Flavius Hence! home, you idle creatures, get you home!
  Is this a holiday? What, know you not,
  Being mechanical, you ought not to walk
  Upon a labouring day without the sign
  Of your profession? Speak, what trade art thou?   5

Carpenter Why sir, a carpenter.

Marullus Where is thy leather apron and thy rule?
  What dost thou with thy best apparel on?
  You, sir, what trade are you?

Cobbler Truly sir, in respect of a fine workman, I   10
  am but, as you would say, a cobbler.

Marullus But what trade art thou? Answer me
  directly.

Cobbler A trade, sir, that I hope I may use with a
  safe conscience, which is indeed, sir, a mender of   15
  bad soles.

Flavius What trade, thou knave? Thou naughty
  knave, what trade?

Cobbler Nay, I beseech you sir, be not out with me,
  yet if thou be out, sir, I can mend you.   20

Marullus What mean'st thou by that? Mend me,
  thou saucy fellow?

Cobbler Why, sir, cobble you.

NOTES

S.D. *over the stage:* the commoners cross the stage before halting. In most productions, they enter first, with Flavius and Marullus following them.

3. *Being mechanical:* being artisans or workers.

4–5. *sign / Of your profession:* dress or symbol of your trade.

11. *cobbler:* this means bungler as well as shoemaker and confuses Marullus. The cobbler puns throughout his speeches.

16. *soles:* of shoes, with a pun on soul.

17. *naughty:* insolent. A stronger term for the Elizabethans than for us today.

knave: base and crafty rogue.

19. *out:* angry.

20. *out:* have shoes out at the sole, or worn out.

23. *cobble you:* hit with stones

Flavius Thou art a cobbler, art thou?

Cobbler Truly sir, all that I live by is with the awl.   25
I meddle with no tradesman's matters nor women's
matters, but withal — I am indeed, sir, a surgeon to
old shoes. When they are in great danger, I recover
them. As proper men as ever trod upon neat's leather
have gone upon my handiwork.   30

Flavius But wherefore art not in thy shop to-day?
Why dost thou lead these men about the streets?

Cobbler Truly sir, to wear out their shoes, to get
myself into more work. But indeed sir, we make holiday to see Caesar and to rejoice in his triumph.   35

Marullus Wherefore rejoice? What conquest brings
     he home?
What tributaries follow him to Rome?
To grace in captive bonds his chariot wheels?
You blocks, you stones, you worse than senseless
     things!
O you hard hearts, you cruel men of Rome!   40
Knew you not Pompey? Many a time and oft
Have you climbed up to walls and battlements,
To towers and windows, yea, to chimney tops,
Your infants in your arms, and there have sat
The livelong day, with patient expectation,   45
To see great Pompey pass the streets of Rome.
And when you saw his chariot but appear,
Have you not made an universal shout,
That Tiber trembled underneath her banks
To hear the replication of your sounds   50
Made in her concave shores?
And do you now put-on your best attire?
And do you now cull out a holiday?
And do you now strew flowers in his way
That comes in triumph over Pompey's blood?   55
Be gone!
Run to your houses, fall upon your knees,
Pray to the gods to intermit the plague
That needs must light on this ingratitude.

Flavius Go, go, good countrymen, and for this fault   60
Assemble all the poor men of your sort;

25–28. The cobbler continues to have verbal fun at the expense of Flavius and Marullus. Here he says that he is above "meddling" with trade, or ordinary work, just as he is above pursuing women. He gives himself the grandiose title of surgeon "withal," i.e., a surgeon with an awl. In mending or re-covering shoes he makes them "recover," or heals them.

29. *neat's leather:* oxhide.

35. *triumph:* a triumphal procession through Rome. Caesar is returning from the defeat of Pompey's sons in Spain.

37. *tributaries:* conquered rulers bringing tributes of money.

43–49. Here Shakespeare combines the London of his audience ("towers, windows, chimney tops") with the Rome of Pompey's chariot and the river Tiber.

50. *replication:* echo, reverberation.

51. *concave shores:* overhanging banks

53. *Cull out:* choose to take. This is meant ironically, since the artisans could not choose their own holidays.

55. *Pompey's blood:* the blood of Pompey's sons and his armies.

58. *intermit:* hold off.

Draw them to Tiber banks, and weep your tears
Into the channel, till the lowest stream
Do kiss the most exalted shores of all.

[*Exeunt the commoners.*]
See, whe'r their basest mettle be not moved.   65
They vanish tongue-tied in their guiltiness.
Go you down that way towards the Capitol;
This way will I. Disrobe the images
If you do find them decked with ceremonies.

Marullus May we do so?   70
You know it is the feast of Lupercal.

Flavius It is no matter. Let no images
Be hung with Caesar's trophies. I'll about
And drive away the vulgar from the streets.
So do you too, where you perceive them thick.   75
These growing feathers, plucked from Caesar's wing
Will make him fly an ordinary pitch,
Who else would soar above the view of men
And keep us all in servile fearfulness.

[*Exeunt.*]

64.   *most exalted shores:* highest banks.

65.   *whe'r:* frequent in Shakespeare for whether.

      mettle: temperament, disposition.

      moved: affected, changed; i.e., to guilt at forgetting Pompey.

67.   *Capitol:* the Temple of Jupiter on the Capitoline Hill where the state business of Rome was transacted.

68.   *images:* statues.

69.   *ceremonies:* ornaments such as garlands or wreaths.

74.   *the vulgar:* the common people.

76–79.   The image is from falconry, with Caesar as the falcon whose "wing" (power) will be weaker if his "growing feathers" (popular support) are plucked, causing him to fly at a lower "pitch" (height).

COMMENTARY

The play opens on a scene of raucous public celebration. Not only is it February 15, the Feast of the Lupercal, but it is also the day Julius Caesar triumphantly returns from Spain after defeating the last of Rome's external adversaries. The crowd of revelers is happy to have a day away from their usual tasks and, because the day is considered a high festival, plenty of government-supplied food and drink is available for all.

The Lupercalian holiday, an ancient rite of both purgation and fertility, honored the gods Lupercus and Faunus as well as the twin brothers Romulus and Remus, the legendary founders of Rome. It seems appropriate that Shakespeare chose this particular feast as the setting for the return of Julius Caesar to Rome. Historically, Caesar returned from Spain in October of 45 B.C., but by dramatically compressing the events, Shakespeare draws a comparison between Romulus and Remus, the founders of Rome, and Caesar, the founder of a new Roman order. By implication, the religious festival, combined with Caesar's ceremonial entrance into the city, gives Caesar an immediate godlike aura and would possibly remind the viewer of Jesus' triumphant entrance into Jerusalem before his betrayal and death on the cross.

The merriment of the Roman people is short-lived, however, as the scene is quickly broken up by the intrusion of two Roman Tribunes, Marullus and Flavius. The two men insult the crowd and admonish them for being idle on a workday. They also question why the commoners walk about "without the sign of your profession." This is a reference to an Elizabethan law that required workers to identify themselves by wearing their work clothes and carrying the tools of their trade. Shakespeare often used Elizabethan references in his plays, regardless of the actual timeframe in which the story was taking place, as a way of making his work more accessible to his audience. Another example of Shakespeare using Elizabethan references in this scene

A relief of Romulus and Remus, from the 1st century, A.D. Mark Smith/Ancient Art & Architecture Collection Ltd.

is the reference to towers and chimney tops. There were no towers or chimneys in ancient Rome, but these anachronisms, chronologically misplaced events, words or details, bring the play into alignment with the experiences of the audience for whom the play was written.

Shakespeare wrote the majority of his plays in blank verse, but he often changed from verse to prose to indicate the social status of a character. In this scene, the tribunes speak verse and the commoners use prose. In a delightful bit of wordplay, the Carpenter and the Cobbler frustrate the Tribunes with their evasive puns and bawdy innuendoes. *Puns,* a play on words that are spelled or sound the same but have different meanings, have often been called the lowest form of humor, but Elizabethan audiences delighted in them.

In general, the crowd is content with the harmony and abundance in their lives and is more concerned with parties than with politics. Infuriated by the mob's indifference, Marullus questions the crowd's memories and motivations. How is Caesar's returning from the defeat of another Roman a victory? Marullus also underscores the fickleness of the people by reminding them that it was not so long ago that they stood in the very same place celebrating the return of Pompey but now celebrate the return of the man who, "comes in triumph over Pompey's blood." The Tribunes scold the onlookers and suggest that the gods should send a plague for this type of ingratitude and the chastised crowd silently and guiltily disperses.

The conflict between the factions of commoner and official serves two dramatic functions. First, Shakespeare puts the central conflict of the play into place.

Although the majority of the people of Rome are happy with their leader, some are not. This small-scale conflict will be reflected in the next scene when the full-blown conspiracy against Caesar begins to take shape. Shakespeare also uses the first scene in the play to establish "the mob" as a character with its own life and set of characteristics, who can be moved to change its mind about an issue with a few well-chosen words.

Finally, the scene introduces one of the many images that enhances the play as well as one of the play's recurring themes. The word "blood," implying the dual meaning of "life-nourishing" and "death-inducing," is used consistently throughout the play. Here, Caesar has triumphed over Pompey's blood, but there will soon be a time when Caesar's body, lying bloody at the base of Pompey's statue, will be triumphed by Pompey. This image illustrates a theme in *Julius Caesar,* that blood begets blood.

The birth of Julius Caesar. Ronald Sheridan/Ancient Art & Architecture Collection Ltd.

Act I, Scene 2

Caesar enters with his procession, which includes, among others, his wife Calpurnia and Marc Antony. Caesar is accosted by a soothsayer who warns him to "Beware the Ides of March." Caesar dismisses the man as a dreamer and moves on to begin the festivities for the Feast Day. Left behind are two men, Brutus and Cassius. Cassius strikes up a conversation with Brutus and learns that Brutus is not happy with Caesar's sharp rise to power. Cassius, also wary of Caesar's power, attempts to enlist support from Brutus in an effort to do something about Caesar before the people crown him king, giving him absolute power. While Brutus and Cassius are having this conversation, shouts are heard from offstage. Antony has offered the crown to Caesar and he has refused it in a ploy to make the people of Rome beg him to take the crown. Instead, the people cheer his decision and Caesar is forced to reject the crown a total of three times. The anger he must suppress causes Caesar to suffer an epileptic seizure. Cassius uses Caesar's weaknesses to persuade Brutus to join in the conspiracy against Caesar. The two men agree to meet at a later time to discuss the matter more fully.

ACT I, SCENE 2.
Rome, a public place.

[*Flourish. Enter* CAESAR, ANTONY (for the course),
　CALPURNIA, PORTIA, DECIUS, CICERO, BRUTUS,
　CASSIUS, CASCA, *a great crowd following, among them a*
　Soothsayer; after them, MARULLUS *and* FLAVIUS]

Caesar Calpurnia.

Casca　　　　　　Peace, ho! Caesar speaks.

Caesar　　　　　　　　　　　　Calpurnia.

Calpurnia Here, my lord.

Caesar Stand you directly in Antonius' way
　When he doth run his course. Antonius.

Antony Caesar, my lord?　　　　　　　　　　　　5

Caesar Forget not in your speed, Antonius,
　To touch Calpurnia; for our elders say
　The barren, touched in this holy chase,

NOTES

S.D.　　*Flourish:* an extended sounding of trumpets, used on the Elizabethan stage to announce the entrance of a procession, or of a ruler and his court. A "sennet" (I.2.24) was a briefer version.

S.D.　　*for the course:* stripped for running.

3.　　*Antonius:* Shakespeare occasionally alters the form of names to maintain the rhythm of the iambic pentameter verse. Here he needs an extra syllable, but compare line 204, below.

Shake off their sterile curse.

Antony I shall remember
When Caesar says 'Do this,' it is performed. 10

Caesar Set on, and leave no ceremony out.

[*Flourish.*]

Soothsayer Caesar!

Caesar Ha! Who calls?

Casca Bid every noise be still. Peace yet again!

Caesar Who is it in the press that calls on me? 15
I hear a tongue shriller than all the music
Cry 'Caesar!' Speak. Caesar is turned to hear.

Soothsayer Beware the ides of March.

Caesar What man is that?

Brutus A soothsayer bids you beware the ides of March.

Caesar Set him before me; let me see his face. 20

Cassius Fellow, come from the throng; look upon Caesar.

Caesar What say'st thou to me now? Speak once again.

Soothsayer Beware the ides of March.

Caesar He is a dreamer. Let us leave him. Pass.

[*Sennet. Exeunt all except* BRUTUS *and* CASSIUS.]

Cassius Will you go see the order of the course? 25

Brutus Not I.

Cassius I pray you do.

Brutus I am not gamesome. I do lack some part
Of that quick spirit that is in Antony.
Let me not hinder, Cassius, your desires. 30
I'll leave you.

Cassius Brutus, I do observe you now of late;
I have not from your eyes that gentleness
And show of love as I was wont to have.
You bear too stubborn and too strange a hand 35
Over your friend that loves you.

15. *press:* crowd.

18. *ides:* the fifteenth day of the month.

25. *order:* sequence of events.

28. *gamesome:* sportive.

29. *quick:* light, lively. The evidence that Brutus is troubled by Caesar's threat to republican freedom appears early in the scene and Cassius is quick to note it.

33. *I . . . eyes:* i.e., I do not see in your eyes.

35–36. *You . . . friend:* the metaphor is from riding. Cassius says that Brutus handles him too roughly.

Brutus   Cassius,
  Be not deceived. If I have veiled my look,
  I turn the trouble of my countenance
  Merely upon myself. Vexed I am
  Of late with passions of some difference,   40
  Conceptions only proper to myself,
  Which give some soil, perhaps, to my behaviours;
  But let not therefore my good friends be grieved
  (Among which number, Cassius, be you one)
  Nor construe any further my neglect   45
  Than that poor Brutus, with himself at war,
  Forgets the shows of love to other men.

Cassius Then, Brutus, I have much mistook your
     passion;
  By means wherof this breast of mine hath buried
  Thoughts of great value, worthy cogitations.   50
  Tell me, good Brutus, can you see your face?

Brutus No, Cassius; for the eye sees not itself
  But by reflection, by some other things.

Cassius 'Tis just.
  And it is very much lamented, Brutus,   55
  That you have no such mirrors as will turn
  Your hidden worthiness into your eye,
  That you might see your shadow. I have heard
  Where many of the best respect in Rome,
  (Except immortal Caesar), speaking of Brutus,   60
  And groaning underneath this age's yoke,
  Have wished that noble Brutus had his eyes.

Brutus Into what dangers would you lead me,
     Cassius,
  That you would have me seek into myself
  For that which is not in me?   65

Cassius Therefore, good Brutus, be prepared to
     hear;
  And since you know you cannot see yourself
  So well as by reflection, I, your glass,
  Will modestly discover to yourself
  That of yourself which you yet know not of.   70
  And be not jealous on me, gentle Brutus.

37–39.   *If . . . myself:* i.e., if I have seemed unfriendly, it is because I am concerned with my own thoughts.

39.   *Merely:* wholly.

40.   *passions . . . difference:* conflicting emotions.

41.   *proper:* belonging.

42.   *soil:* blemish.

45.   *construe:* understand (with the accent on the first syllable).

48.   *passion:* emotion.

49.   *By . . . buried:* i.e., I have therefore concealed.

59.   *best respect:* highest reputation.

60.   *(Except immortal Caesar):* spoken with quiet irony; Cassius begins to be specific about what he thinks is amiss in Rome.

62.   *Brutus . . . eyes:* i.e., that Brutus saw where he himself stood; not blind to the situation.

68.   *glass:* mirror

69.   *modestly:* without exaggeration.

71.   *jealous:* suspicious.

Were I a common laughter, or did use
To stale with ordinary oaths my love
To every new protester; if you know
That I do fawn on men and hug them hard,   75
And after scandal them; or if you know
That I profess myself in banqueting
To all the rout, then hold me dangerous.

[*Flourish and shout.*]

Brutus What means this shouting? I do fear the people
Choose Caesar for their king.   80

Cassius   Ay, do you fear it?
Then must I think you would not have it so.

Brutus I would not Cassius; yet I love him well.
But wherefore do you hold me here so long?
What is it that you would impart to me?
If it he aught toward the general good,   85
Set honour in one eye and death i' th' other,
And I will look on both indifferently;
For let the gods so speed me as I love
The name of honour more than I fear death.

Cassius I know that virtue to be in you, Brutus,   90
As well as I do know your outward favour.
Well, honour is the subject of my story.
I cannot tell what you and other men
Think of this life; but for my single self,
I had as lief not be as live to be   95
In awe of such a thing as I myself.
I was borne free as Caesar; so were you.
We both have fed as well, and we can both
Endure the winter's cold as well as he.
For once, upon a raw and gusty day,   100
The troubled Tiber chafing with her shores,
Caesar said to me, 'Dar'st thou, Cassius, now
Leap in with me into this angry flood
And swim to yonder point?' Upon the word,
Accoutred as I was, I plunged in   105
And bade him follow. So indeed he did.
The torrent roared, and we did buffet it
With lusty sinews, throwing it aside

---

72.   *laughter:* object of laughter or ridicule. Some editors print "laugher".

73.   *stale:* cheapen.

     ordinary: a tavern/common

74.   *new protester:* i.e., every newcomer who declares his friendship.

75.   *fawn:* physical gesture

76.   *scandal:* slander.

77–78.   *profess . . . rout:* proclaim my friendship to everyone ("all the rout") while celebrating.

78.   *dangerous:* unreliable, unable to keep secrets.

S.D.   *shout:* here and at line 132 dramatically reminds Brutus and Cassius (and the audience) of Caesar's popularity with the mob.

87.   *indifferently:* impartially, with equal favor.

88.   *so . . . as:* assist me because.

96.   *such . . . myself:* i.e., another man like myself, in this case Caesar.

101.   *chafing with:* beating on.

105.   *accoutred:* in armor.

107.   *buffet:* beat back.

108.   *lusty sinews:* strong muscles.

And stemming it with hearts of controversy.
But ere we could arrive the point proposed,   110
Caesar cried, 'Help me Cassius, or I sink!'
I, as Aeneas, our great ancestor,
Did from the flames of Troy upon his shoulder
The old Anchises bear, so from the waves of Tiber
Did I the tired Caesar. And this man   115
Is now become a god, and Cassius is
A wretched creature and must bend his body
If Caesar carelessly but nod on him.
He had a fever when he was in Spain,
And when the fit was on him, I did mark   120
How he did shake. 'Tis true, this god did shake.
His coward lips did from their colour fly,
And that same eye whose bend doth awe the world
Did lose his lustre. I did hear him groan.
Ay, and that tongue of his that bade the Romans   125
Mark him and write his speeches in their books,
'Alas,' it cried, 'give me some drink, Titinius,'
As a sick girl! Ye gods, it doth amaze me
A man of such a feeble temper should
So get the start of the majestic world   130
And bear the palm alone.

[*Shout. Flourish.*]

Brutus Another general shout?
I do believe that these applauses are
For some new honours that are heaped on Caesar.

Cassius Why, man, he doth bestride the narrow   135
    world
Like a Colossus, and we petty men
Walk under his huge legs and peep about
To find ourselves dishonourable graves.
Men at some time are masters of their fates.
The fault, dear Brutus, is not in our stars,   140
But in ourselves, that we are underlings.
'Brutus,' and 'Caesar.' What should be in that
    'Caesar'?
Why should that name be sounded more than yours?
Write them together: yours is as fair a name.
Sound them: it doth become the mouth as well.   145
Weigh them: It is as heavy. Conjure with 'em:

---

109. *hearts of controversy:* in rivalry.

117. *bend:* bow in reverence.

130. *get the start:* i.e., a head start; the metaphor from the running of a race is carried on in the victor's "palm" in the next line.

136. *Colossus:* the huge statue of Apollo at the harbour of Rhodes. It was erroneously thought that its legs spanned the harbour entrance.

143. *sounded:* proclaimed.

146. *conjure:* pronounce as in a spell.

'Brutus' will start a spirit as soon as 'Caesar.'
Now in the names of all the gods at once,
Upon what meat doth this our Caesar feed
That he is grown so great? Age thou art shamed.   150
Rome, thou hast lost the breed of noble bloods.
When went there by an age since the great Flood
But it was famed with more than with one man?
When could they say (till now) that talked of Rome
That her wide walks encompassed but one man?   155
Now is it Rome indeed, and room enough,
When there is in it but one only man.
O, you and I have heard our fathers say
There was a Brutus once that would have brooked
Th' eternal devil to keep his state in Rome   160
As easily as a king.

Brutus That you do love me I am nothing jealous.
What you would work me to, I have some aim.
How I have thought of this, and of these times,
I shall recount hereafter. For this present,   165
I would not so (with love I might entreat you)
Be any further moved. What you have said
I will consider; what you have to say
I will with patience hear, and find a time
Both meet to hear and answer such high things.   170
Till then, my noble friend, chew upon this:
Brutus had rather be a villager
Than to repute himself a son of Rome
Under these hard conditions as this time
Is like to lay upon us.   175

Cassius   I am glad
That my weak words have struck but thus much
    show
Of fire from Brutus.

[*Enter* CAESAR *and his train.*]

Brutus The games are done, and Caesar is returning.

Cassius As they pass by, pluck Casca by the sleeve,
And he will (after his sour fashion) tell you   180
What hath proceeded worthy note to-day.

Brutus I will do so. But look you, Cassius,

---

147.   *start:* invoke, as in a prayer to a god.

152.   *great Flood:* the classical or pagan version of Noah's Flood.

153.   *But . . . man:* i.e., has there ever been another age in which a single man has been in this position?

155.   *walks:* public parks and gardens that have become (Cassius suggests) Caesar's private preserve.

156.   *Rome . . . room:* these words were pronounced alike by the Elizabethans, and Cassius' pun is meant to suggest that all of Rome is now the single "room" of one man.

159–61.   i.e., would no more have permitted a king in Rome than a devil.

162.   *nothing jealous:* have no doubt. The Elizabethans frequently used "jealous" in the sense of suspicious.

166.   *so:* in this manner.

170.   *meet:* proper.

S.D.   *train:* followers.

The angry spot doth glow on Caesar's brow,
And all the rest look like a chidden train.
Calpurnia's cheek is pale, and Cicero   185
Looks with such ferret and such fiery eyes
As we have seen him in the Capitol,
Being crossed in conference by some senators.

Cassius Casca will tell us what the matter is.

Caesar Antonius.   190

Antony Caesar?

Caesar Let me have men about me that are fat,
Sleek-headed men, and such as sleep a-nights.
Yond Cassius has a lean and hungry look.
He thinks too much. Such men are dangerous.   195

Antony Fear him not Caesar; he's not dangerous.
He is a noble Roman, and well given.

Caesar Would he were fatter! But I fear him not.
Yet if my name were liable to fear,
I do not know the man I should avoid   200
So soon as that spare Cassius. He reads much,
He is a great observer, and he looks
Quite through the deeds of men. He loves no plays
As thou dost, Antony; he hears no music.
Seldom he smiles, and smiles in such a sort   205
As if he mocked himself and scorned his spirit
That could be moved to smile at anything.
Such men as he be never at heart's ease
Whiles they behold a greater than themselves,
And therefore are they very dangerous.   210
I rather tell thee what is to be feared
Than what I fear; for always I am Caesar.
Come on my right hand, for this ear is deaf,
And tell me truly what thou think'st of him.

[*Sennet. Exeunt* CAESAR *and his train.* CASCA *remains.*]

Casca You pulled me by the cloak. Would you   215
　　speak with me?

Brutus Ay, Casca. Tell us what hath chanced to-day
That Caesar looks so sad.

Casca Why, you were with him, were you not?

184.　*chidden:* scolded.

186.　*ferret:* red

188.　*crossed:* opposed.

192–94.　Caesar's distinction between "fat" and "lean" repeats the ancient proverbial notion of "fat" as amiable and satisfied, "lean" as dissatisfied and envious.

197.　*well given:* well disposed.

199.　*Yet . . . fear:* if I were capable of being afraid.

203.　*Quite . . . men:* i.e., through their actions and into their motives.

204.　*music:* dislike of music in Shakespeare's plays and for the Elizabethans generally represented a defect, or disharmony of character. Note later in the play Brutus' fondness for music (IV.3).

205.　*sort:* way.

217.　*sad:* troubled.

Brutus I should not then ask Casca what had chanced.

Casca Why, there was a crown offered him; and   220
being offered him, he put it by the back of his hand
thus; and then the people fell a-shouting.

Brutus What was the second noise for?

Casca Why, for that too.

Cassius They shouted thrice. What was the last cry   225
for?

Casca Why, for that too.

Brutus Was the crown offered him thrice?

Casca Ay, marry was't! and he put it by thrice,
every time gentler than other; and at every putting-   230
by mine honest neighbours shouted.

Cassius Who offered him the crown?

Casca Why, Antony.

Brutus Tell us the manner of it, gentle Casca.

Casca I can as well be hanged as tell the manner   235
of it. It was mere foolery; I did not mark it. I saw
Mark Antony offer him a crown — yet 'twas not a
crown neither, 'twas one of these coronets — and, as
I told you, he put it by once; but for all that, to my
thinking, he would fain have had it. Then he offered   240
it to him again; then he put it by again; but to my
thinking, he was very loath to lay his fingers off it.
And then he offered it the third time. He put it the
third time by; and still as he refused it, the rabble-
ment hooted, and clapped their chopt hands, and   245
threw tip their sweaty nightcaps, and uttered such a
deal of stinking breath because Caesar refused the
crown that it had almost choked Caesar; for he
swounded and fell down at it. And for mine own
part, I durst not laugh, for fear of opening my lips   250
and receiving the bad air.

Cassius But soft, I pray you. What, did Caesar
swound?

---

229.   *marry:* an oath, by (the Virgin) Mary.

234.   *gentle:* used here in two senses, (1) noble, or well-born, and (2) mild or amiable (ironic when applied to the "sour" Casca).

238.   *coronets:* small crown, or perhaps a laurel wreath.

240.   *fain:* gladly.

245.   *chopt:* chapped.

249.   *swounded:* fainted.

252.   *But soft:* slowly/just a moment.

Casca He fell down in the market place and foamed
at the mouth and was speechless.   255

Brutus 'Tis very like; he hath the falling sickness.

Cassius No, Caesar hath it not; but you and I,
And honest Casca, we have the falling sickness.

Casca I know not what you mean by that, but I
am sure Caesar fell down. If the rag-tag people did   260
not clap him and hiss him, according as he pleased
and displeased them, as they use to do the players
in the theatre, I am no true man.

Brutus What said he when he came unto himself?

Casca Marry, before he fell down, when lie per-   265
ceived the common herd was glad he refused the
crown, he plucked me ope his doublet and offered
them his throat to cut. An I had been a man of any
occupation, if I would not have taken him at a word,
I would I might go to hell among the rogues. And so   270
he fell. When he came to himself again, he said, if
he had done or said anything amiss, he desired their
worships to think it was his infirmity. Three or
four wenches where I stood cried 'Alas, good soul!'
and forgave him with all their hearts. But there's no   275
heed to be taken of them. If Caesar had stabbed
their mothers, they would have done no less.

Brutus And after that, he came thus sad away?

Casca Ay.

Cassius Did Cicero say anything?   280

Casca Ay, he spoke Greek.

Cassius To what effect?

Casca Nay, an I tell you that, I'll ne'er look you i'
the face again. But those that understood him
smiled at one another and shook their heads; but   285
for mine own part, it was Greek to me. I could tell
you more news too. Marullus and Flavius, for pull-
ing scarfs off Caesar's images, are put to silence.
Fare you well. There was more foolery yet, if I could
remember it.   290

256. *falling sickness:* Brutus refers to Caesar's epilepsy. Cassius is quick to take up the phrase and give it another meaning. They are "falling" through Caesar's rise.

260. *rag-tag:* ragged.

267. *plucked me ope:* opened. Caesar wants to assure the crowd of his sincerity.

269. *occupation:* working man.

286. *Greek to me:* In fact, Plutarch says specifically that Casca could speak Greek. In this phrase (which has become a part of the language), Shakespeare makes Casca disclaim any knowledge that might make him appear sophisticated or polished. He maintains his rough-hewn "blunt" and "sour" character. See Brutus' and Cassius' comments at line 298 ff. below.

288. *put to silence:* a euphemism for executed.

Cassius Will you sup with me to-night, Casca?

Casca No, I am promised forth.

Cassius Will you dine with me to-morrow?

Casca Ay, if I be alive, and your mind hold, and
your dinner worth eating.   295

Cassius Good. I will expect you.

Casca Do so. Farewell both. [*Exit.*]

Brutus What a blunt fellow is this grown to be!
He was quick mettle when he went to school.

Cassius So is he now in execution   300
Of any bold or noble enterprise,
However he puts on this tardy form.
This rudeness is a sauce to his good wit,
Which gives men stomach to digest his words
With better appetite.   305

Brutus And so it is. For this time I will leave you.
To-morrow, if you please to speak with me,
I will come home to you; or if you will,
Come home to me, and I will wait for you.

Cassius I will do so. Till then, think of the world.   310

[*Exit* BRUTUS.]
Well, Brutus, thou art noble; yet I see
Thy honourable mettle may be wrought
From that it is disposed. Therefore it is meet
That noble minds keep ever with their likes;
For who so firm that cannot be seduced?   315
Caesar doth bear me hard; but he loves Brutus.
If I were Brutus now and he were Cassius,
He should not humour me. I will this night,
In several hands, in at his windows throw,
As if they came from several citizens,   320
Writings, all tending to the great opinion
That Rome holds of his name; wherein obscurely
Caesar's ambition shall be glanced at.
And after this let Caesar seat him sure,
For we will shake him, or worse days endure. [*Exit.*]   325

294. *your mind hold:* (1) if you don't change your mind, (2) if you are still sane.

299. *quick mettle:* sharp.

302. *puts . . . form:* pretends to be slow and simple.

310. *the world:* i.e., the Roman world.

312. *wrought:* worked on, changed.

313. *that . . . disposed:* its natural inclination.

314. *with their likes:* with those that think as they do.

316. *bear me hard:* bears me a grudge.

318. *humour:* persuade by flattery. Lines 317–318 have been variously interpreted. They may mean (1) If I were Brutus and Brutus were Cassius, he would not persuade me, or (2) If I were Brutus and Caesar were Cassius, Caesar would not persuade me. The interpretation is of some importance. The first, which seems also the likeliest, puts Cassius (at least at this point in the play) in a particularly cynical and cold-blooded light.

319. *several hands:* different handwritings.

321–2. *great opinion / That:* great respect in which.

323. *ambition:* for the Elizabethans, the word had the special meaning of unscrupulous pursuit of power.

glanced at: hinted at.

COMMENTARY

The disparity between the public image and the private man is central to *Julius Caesar*, and this introduction to Caesar certainly underscores Shakespeare's ability to understand and portray the complex and often dual nature of human beings. Despite the debate that has raged for years over who is the actual "hero" of *Julius Caesar*, no clear-cut protagonist ever emerges in the play. The simplistic beauty of this drama lies in the fact that, just like life off of the stage, politicians and public figures, no matter how the populace chooses to see them, are mere mortals with the same ailments and torments, delusions and misjudgments as the common person.

A great flourish of trumpets signals the arrival of Caesar and his entourage. A large crowd of people that includes both friends and foes accompanies him. Although they speak no lines and are never referred to, the stage directions indicate that Marullus and Flavius, the chastising tribunes from the previous scene, are part of this crowd, possibly as prisoners having already been arrested for desecrating Caesar's statues. The two men in chains would serve as a potent visual image of Caesar's power and control over attempts to undermine his authority. Also in the crowd are Caesar's right-hand man, Marc Antony, and the men who will become the prevailing forces of the conspiracy against Caesar.

Marc Antony, also known as Marcus Antonius, was related to Julius Caesar on his mother's side. He had been a staunch supporter of Caesar during the conflicts with Pompey and had served in Caesar's army when he was in Gaul. In Scene 2, Antony is dressed "for the course." As indicated in Scene 1, it is the Feast of the

Julius Caesar depicted as a deity in his chariot.
Mary Evans Picture Library

Lupercal. During the holiday, priests of the Lupercus, dressed in loincloths made of goatskin, sacrificed goats and a dog and smeared themselves with sacrificial blood. They then ran through the city carrying a goatskin thong, called a *februa*. Women placed themselves in such a way that the priests could strike them with the februa, thus assuring the women of fertility and easy childbirth. In this short exchange, Shakespeare makes apparent Antony's exalted position not only as a priest of the Luperci but as a loyal and dedicated follower of Caesar. When asked to touch Calpurnia with his thong, Antony's reply, "When Caesar says 'Do this,' it is performed," explicitly defines the depth of his allegiance to the leader of Rome.

Caesar's first words are directed at his wife, Calpurnia. She is Caesar's third wife and the daughter of a friend of Pompey's, indicating that the marriage was most likely politically motivated. Indeed, a young, healthy bride should have been able to produce the heir that Caesar surely desires to guarantee the continuation of his reign as leader of Rome. Caesar's rather brazen public acknowledgment of Calpurnia's sterility gives several clues to Caesar's character and his motivations. First, he must maintain his own public image by degrading Calpurnia. In an insensitive and rather humiliating manner, Caesar seems to place the blame for their lack of children on his wife. However, the "sterile curse" *could* be Caesar's own aging impotence that prevents Calpurnia from becoming pregnant. According to Plutarch, Shakespeare's main source for much of this play, "The chiefest cause that made [Caesar] mortally hated was the covetous desire he had to be called king." Caesar's obvious desire to produce a male heir may indicate that Caesar was indeed thinking along those lines.

Just as Caesar makes it obvious that he believes in the superstition attached to the Lupercal to cure Calpurnia of her supposed sterility, the procession is interrupted by the warnings of a soothsayer, a man who sees into the future. Both the Romans of Caesar's time and the Elizabethans who saw the play enacted on the stage of The Globe were very superstitious and would have appreciated the import of prophecies, dreams, and omens, and anticipated the dire results when those

signs were ignored. Here, Caesar is warned to "Beware the Ides of March," but despite the fact that he has proven to be a superstitious man when it pertains to others, he chooses to ignore the warning and dismisses the soothsayer as nothing more than a dreamer. Ironically, Cassius, the man who repeats the soothsayer's warning to Caesar, is the very man who will help to make the prophecy come true.

Caesar's brief exchange with the soothsayer provides more insights into Caesar's character. He is a man who will tempt the fates by ignoring the messages passed to him by the soothsayer. In essence, Caesar seems to have put himself on a par with the gods, in control of destiny as opposed to being controlled by it. This arrogance would have been a red flag to Elizabethan audiences that Caesar was setting himself up for a mighty fall from grace. Also, Caesar's use of the third person when referring to himself suggests that Caesar has begun to believe his own press. The references to himself combined with his disregard of prophecy point to the fact that Caesar is actively participating in his own deification.

Followed by the crowd, Caesar leaves the stage to watch the race. Two men, Brutus and Cassius, lag behind and, left alone on stage, begin a dialogue that will change the course of history. Marcus Junius Brutus, born in 85 B.C., was a nephew of Cato, one of Caesar's most unyielding adversaries. As Cato's nephew, Brutus was considered an enemy of Caesar. He fought with Pompey in Greece and was taken prisoner when Pompey was defeated. In an effort to heal the wounds of civil war, Caesar pardoned and set free the prisoners of war, including Brutus. Shortly thereafter, Brutus became a lieutenant in Caesar's army and continued to serve him loyally. Although Shakespeare makes no direct mention of it in his play, it was common knowledge to most Elizabethans that Brutus' mother, Servilia, had had an affair with Julius Caesar. Because Brutus was born during the time of this relationship, it was speculated that Brutus might have actually been Caesar's illegitimate son.

Brutus subscribed to the philosophy known as *Stoicism,* which maintains that the universe is completely rational and guided by fate. Therefore, one must learn to accept whatever happens with a strong and tranquil mind. Virtue, being the attainment of valor, moral excellence, and righteousness, is the only key to a happy life and becomes the ultimate goal of the Stoic; vice is evil and leads only to unhappiness. Stoicism encourages a man to be centered in his intellect while suppressing his feelings. Brutus' attempt to maintain his emotionless moral superiority, based in his Stoic philosophy, becomes a double-edged sword and ultimately leads him — and Rome — into destruction.

Caius Cassius Longinus was also an ally of Pompey, but when he saw that Pompey's defeat was imminent, he changed allegiance and, after being pardoned by Caesar, became a soldier in Caesar's army. Cassius, married to Brutus' sister Junia, was Brutus's brother-in-law. Unlike the Stoic Brutus, Cassius was an Epicurean. The philosophy of *Epicureanism* promoted the notion that freedom from physical pain and mental trouble was the goal of a happy life. Again, virtue, courage, and justice were considered the attributes needed to attain wisdom, but unlike the intellectual center of stoicism, Epicurians felt that knowledge was derived from the senses. Brutus' cold and unwavering intellect offers a direct contrast to the fiery, passionate nature of Cassius. Thus, as Brutus lived in his head, Cassius lived in his heart. Just as Brutus' inability to balance head and heart will lead to his downfall, Cassius' inability to balance heart and head will also lead to his ruin.

Much of the manipulation that occurs in *Julius Caesar* is achieved by the use of flattery. In this scene, Cassius plies Brutus with praise and compliments. He speaks of Brutus' worthiness and the high respect with which he

is held throughout Rome and offers to mirror or reflect Brutus' honorable qualities for him to see. The mirror as a reflection of the moral nature of man was a common literary device in Renaissance literature, and Shakespeare uses this device to hold the mirror up to the moral nature of man on many occasions throughout his plays. More often than not, however, what is reflected is the discord inherent in man's sinful nature. For example, in *Julius Caesar*, Brutus admits that he is at war against himself. What this internal war consists of is revealed here in Scene 2 when the first flourishes and shouts are heard from the crowd offstage. Brutus admits that he fears the people have chosen Caesar as their king but, in the same breath, swears that he loves the man. By the end of his speech, however, it becomes apparent that, for the determinedly Stoic Brutus, love will never conquer or come before the need to maintain honor.

At the admission of his fears, Cassius leaps at the opportunity to involve Brutus in the conspiracy against Caesar. Taking advantage of Brutus' commitment to

Caesar passing the Rubicon.
Ronald Sheridan/Ancient Art & Architecture Collection Ltd.

honor and virtue, Cassius plays upon those words to draw Brutus more deeply into the conspiracy. By pointing out Caesar's weaknesses and physical imperfections, Cassius seeks to emphasize that Caesar is no better than Brutus is. Cassius continues to build his argument against Caesar by appealing not only to Brutus' sense of patriotism to a free Rome but persists in flattering Brutus with a reference to his valiant ancestor, who was noted for having overthrown King Tarquin and creating the Roman Republic. Cassius' words work their magic and Brutus agrees that he has had similar thoughts and would be willing to discuss the issue further at a safer and more convenient time.

In this scene, Shakespeare once again foreshadows Caesar's death and uses irony to underscore what will become part of the dramatic unity of the play. In speaking of the power inherent in Caesar's name, Cassius says, "Conjure with 'em: / 'Brutus' will start a spirit as soon as 'Caesar'. . . " and indeed the irony is that it will be Brutus, who in killing Caesar, will release his spirit. By conjuring up Caesar's spirit to be unleashed upon the world, Brutus has in reality given the name of "Caesar" more power in death than Caesar might have had in life. Caesar's spirit, which cannot be killed, will dominate the second half of this play. Readers who feel the play should have been called *Marcus Brutus* underestimate the historical significance of Caesar's continuing power even after his death.

In Scene 2, Shakespeare first introduces the image of fire that infuses the play from this point on. Fire, which, like blood, can be either a destructive or a purifying force, represents passion and the ability to inflame or enkindle. In lines 176–177, Brutus personifies the flint that Cassius strikes in an effort to spark some sort of flame to fire the conspiracy against Caesar.

When Caesar reenters the stage, the subdued nature of the crowd, the red face of Caesar, and the pale looks of Calpurnia signal that something of significance has transpired offstage while Brutus and Cassius conversed onstage. Cassius pulls Casca aside to inquire about the events that have just taken place and Caesar notices the men speaking together in whispers. From his insights into Cassius' character, it is evident that Caesar himself is a "great observer" who can "look through the deeds of men," but his pride and vanity will not allow him to admit to the real danger that a man like Cassius could pose.

In this play, most of what is thought to be known about Caesar is secondhand information passed on by his enemies. Through their eyes, a portrait is drawn of a vain and arrogant man who is weak and unyielding. Historically, Julius Caesar was recorded to be an intelligent, witty, and charming man. An excellent orator and a brilliant writer, Caesar brought about much needed reforms in the Roman Senate, instituted the first public library, improved the system of taxation, rebuilt cities, and sought to have laws passed that would strengthen the moral fabric of society. Shakespeare's Caesar reflects little of these redeeming qualities and remains as human and ambiguous as the other characters in the play. Indeed, Shakespeare seems to deliberately balance Caesar's posturing with almost immediate confessions of weakness. For example, in lines 212–213, Caesar proclaims "for always I am Caesar," immediately followed by the admission that he is partially deaf.

Caesar's seizures, as recorded in Plutarch, and his deafness, as invented by Shakespeare, serve a dramatic function as well as being indicators of Caesar's character. Caesar's infirmities become symbolic of, or a metaphor for, the diseases running rampant in Rome. In Shakespeare's time, the Elizabethans were very aware of the existence of the body politic, a way of defining the state in human terms. The leader is the head of the body politic; the people represent the limbs. Just as Caesar's illnesses weaken his constitution, the state's illnesses, such as bipartisanism and civil disorder, weaken the body politic.

Casca reveals to Brutus and Cassius the events that took place off stage and caused such a show of concern from Caesar and his followers. According to the cynical Casca, speaking in plain and straightforward prose, Antony offered a crown of laurel leaves to Caesar, who, in a show of humility, refused it. The crowd so cheered Caesar's refusal of the crown that he had no choice but to continue to refuse the laurel wreath on three separate occasions. In Casca's view, Caesar desperately wanted to accept the crown, and his refusal of it was an act for the adoring crowd. Obviously, with his red face as proof, Caesar was so angered by the crowd's reaction that he suffered an epileptic fit. The common people's love for Caesar grows to a fever pitch. There is a need among the masses for a "Caesar," and for the time being, they are happy and content with this one.

Casca expresses his concern over the events that have just transpired and delivers the news that Marullus and Flavius have been put to death. Casca agrees to meet with Cassius at a later time. Brutus also takes his leave with a promise to ponder further the issues the men have been discussing.

Left alone on stage, Cassius delivers the first soliloquy of the play. A soliloquy is a dramatic device used to allow a character the opportunity to express the real truth behind his thoughts, feelings, and actions. In this speech, Cassius exposes both his *Machiavellian* tendencies (unscrupulous and unprincipled means to achieve a dishonorable end) and his delight in his own deviousness. In his continuing effort to play into Brutus' vanity, Cassius reveals that he will forge several notes and throw them into Brutus' window. These notes will proclaim the respect that Brutus commands in Rome and suggest that others are not satisfied with Caesar as absolute leader. Using a play on words,

Caesar refusing the crown offered him by Antony.
Mary Evans Picture Library

Cassius smugly revels in the fact that Brutus' honorable "mettle" can, with fiery passion and praise, be changed, just like heated metal could be forged into something new. That Cassius must forge the letters reveals that the common people of Rome are content with Caesar as their leader and share none of the concerns of Cassius or the other members of the conspiracy.

Act I, Scene 3

One month passes. It is now the evening of the Ides of March and a storm rages on Rome. Casca meets Cicero on the street and tells him of the strange and eerie sights he has seen. Cassius arrives and Casca gives him the news that the Senate means to crown Caesar king the following day. Now with a heightened sense of urgency, Cassius knows he must pull the forces of the conspiracy together immediately. Cassius enlists Casca into the group of conspirators and makes his way to Brutus' home. Brutus must join the conspiracy if it is to be seen as a noble enterprise.

ACT I, SCENE 3.
Rome, a street.

[Thunder and lightning. Enter, from opposite sides, CASCA
with his Sword drawn, and CICERO.*]*

Cicero Good even, Casca. Brought you Caesar home?
Why are you breathless? and why stare you so?

Casca Are you not moved when all the sway of earth
Shakes like a thing infirm? O Cicero,
I have seen tempests when the scolding winds 5
Have rived the knotty oaks, and I have seen
Th' ambitious ocean swell and rage and foam
To be exalted with the threat'ning clouds;
But never till to-night, never till now,
Did I go through a tempest dropping fire. 10
Either there is a civil strife in heaven,
Or else the world, too saucy with the gods,
Incenses them to send destruction.

Cicero Why, saw you anything more wonderful?

Casca A common slave (you know him well by sight) 15
Held up his left hand, which did flame and burn
Like twenty torches joined; and yet his hand,
Not sensible of fire, remained unscorched.
Besides (I ha' not since put up my sword),
Against the Capitol I met a lion, 20
Who glazed upon me, and went surly by
Without annoying me. And there were drawn
Upon a heap a hundred ghastly women,
Transformed with their fear, who swore they saw
Men, all in fire, walk up and down the streets. 25

NOTES

1. *Brought:* escorted.

3. *sway:* established order.

6. *rived:* split in two.

10. *dropping fire:* thunderbolts. In this and what follows, Shakespeare may be adapting Plutarch's suggestion that, before Caesar's assassination, "divers men were seen going up and down in the fire."

18. *Not sensible:* unable to feel.

21. *glazed:* a combination of glared and gazed.

22–23. *drawn . . . heap:* huddled together.

And yesterday the bird of night did sit
Even at noonday upon the market place,
Hooting and shrieking. When these prodigies
Do so conjointly meet, let not men say
'These are their reasons — they are natural,'   30
For I believe they are portentous things
Unto the climate that they point upon.

Cicero It is indeed a strange-disposed time
But men may construe things after their fashion,
Clean from the purpose of the things themselves.   35
Comes Caesar to the Capitol to-morrow?

Casca He doth; for he did bid Antonius
Send word to you he would be there to-morrow.

Cicero Good night then, Casca. This disturb'd sky
Is not to walk in.   40

Casca   Farewell, Cicero. [*Exit* CICERO.]
[*Enter* CASSIUS.]

Cassius. Who's there?

Casca   A Roman

Cassius   Casca, by your voice.

Casca Your ear is good. Cassius, what night is this!

Cassius A very pleasing night to honest men.

Casca Who ever knew the heavens menace so?

Cassius Those that have known the earth so full
of faults.   45
For my part, I have walked about the streets,
Submitting me unto the perilous night,
And, thus unbraced, Casca, as you see,
Have bared my bosom to the thunder-stone;
And when the cross blue lightning seemed to open   50
The breast of heaven, I did present myself
Even in the aim and very flash of it.

Casca But wherefore did you so much tempt the
heavens?
It is the part of men to fear and tremble
When the most mighty gods by tokens send   55
Such dreadful heralds to astonish us.

26. *bird of night:* the owl, also taken from Plutarch.

28. *prodigies:* unnatural events.

32. *climate:* country or region.

34. *construe:* explain (with the accent on the first syllable).

35. *clean . . . purpose:* at variance with the real meaning.

48. *unbraced:* with doublet untied.

49. *thunder-stone:* thunderbolt, lightning.

50. *cross:* forked.

54. *part:* natural action.

56. *astonish:* to stun (originally, with a stone), to terrify.

Cassius You are dull, Casca, and those sparks of
    life
That should be in a Roman you do want,
Or else you use not. You look pale, and gaze,
And put on fear, and cast yourself in wonder,   60
To see the strange impatience of the heavens;
But if you would consider the true cause —
Why all these fires, why all these gliding ghosts,
Why birds and beasts, from quality and kind;
Why old men, fools, and children calculate;   65
Why all these things change from their ordinance,
Their natures, and preformed faculties.
To monstrous quality — why you shall find
That heaven hath infused them with these spirits
To make them instruments of fear and warning   70
Unto some monstrous state.
Now could I, Casca, name to thee a man
Most like this dreadful night
That thunders, lightens, opens graves, and roars
As doth the lion in the Capitol;   75
A man no mightier than thyself or me
In personal action, yet prodigious grown
And fearful, as these strange eruptions are.

Casca 'Tis Caesar that you mean. Is it not, Cassius?

Cassius Let it be who it is. For Romans now   80
Have thews and limbs like to their ancestors;
But woe the while! our fathers' minds are dead,
And we are governed with other mothers' spirits;
Our yoke and sufferance show us womanish.

Casca Indeed, they say the senators to-morrow   85
Mean to establish Caesar as a king,
And he shall wear his crown by sea and land
In every place save here in Italy.

Cassius I know where I will wear this dagger then;
Cassius from bondage will deliver Cassius.   90
Therein, ye gods, you make the weak most strong;
Therein, ye gods, you tyrants do defeat.
Nor stony tower, nor walls of beaten brass,
Nor airless dungeon, nor strong links of iron,
Can be retentive to the strength of spirit;   95

60. *cast . . . wonder:* throw yourself into a state of wonder.

64. *from . . . kind:* changed in their nature.

65. *calculate:* make prophecies.

66. *ordinance:* natural order.

67. *preformed:* innate.

68. *monstrous:* unnatural.

71. *Unto . . . state:* of some terrible happening.

81. *thews:* muscles.

82. *woe the while:* alas for this age.

84. *yoke and sufferance:* i.e., meek endurance of tyranny.

88. *In . . . Italy:* i.e., anywhere in the Roman Empire except Italy itself (which would presumably still be too powerfully republican to permit this).

89. *I . . . then:* i.e., he will sheathe it in his own body.

91. *therein:* i.e., in suicide.

95. *Can . . . to:* can confine.

But life, being weary of these worldly bars,
Never lacks power to dismiss itself.
If I know this, know all the world besides,
That part of tyranny that I do bear
I can shake off at pleasure. [*Thunder still.*]   100

Casca   So can I.
So every bondman in his own hand bears
The power to cancel his captivity.

Cassius And why should Caesar be a tyrant then?
Poor man! I know he would not be a wolf
But that he sees the Romans are but sheep;   105
He were no lion, were not Romans hinds.
Those that with haste will make a mighty fire
Behind it with weak straws. What trash is Rome,
What rubbish and what offal, when it serves
For the base matter to illuminate   110
So vile a thing as Caesar! But, O grief,
Where hast thou led me? I, perhaps, speak this
Before a willing bondman. Then I know
My answer must be made. But I am armed,
And dangers are to me indifferent.   115

Casca You speak to Casca, and to such a man
That is no fleering telltale. Hold, my hand.
Be factious for redress of all these griefs,
And I will set this foot of mine as far
As who goes farthest. [*They shake hands.*]   120

Cassius   There's a bargain made.
Now know you, Casca, I have moved already
Some certain of the noblest-minded Romans
To undergo with me an enterprise
Of honourable dangerous consequence;
And I do know, by this, they stay for me   125
In Pompey's Porch; for now, this fearful night,
There is no stir or walking in the streets,
And the complexion of the element
Is fev'rous, like the work we have in hand,
Most bloody, fiery, and most terrible.   130

[*Enter* CINNA.]

Casca Stand close awhile, for here comes one in
        haste.

98. *know . . . world:* let all the world know.

101. *bondman:* slave.

106. *hinds:* deer, with an Elizabethan pun on servants.

109. *offal:* waste.

110. *illuminate:* give light to, in the sense of making famous.

114. *My . . . made:* i.e., I shall have to defend what I have said.

115. *indifferent:* a matter of indifference.

117. *fleering:* the Elizabethan meaning combined our fawning and sneering.

118. *redress:* rectify a wrong.
     factious: active.

125. *by this:* i.e., because of the storm.

126. *Pompey's Porch:* the colonnade of the theater built by Pompey.

128. *complexion . . . element:* appearance of the sky.

129. *fev'rous:* feverish.

131. *Stand close:* stand back, conceal yourself.

Cassius 'Tis Cinna. I do know him by his gait.
He is a friend. Cinna, where haste you so?

Cinna To find out you. Who's that? Metellus
Cimber?

Cinna No, it is Casca, one incorporate   135
To our attempts. Am I not stayed for, Cinna?

Cinna I am glad on't. What a fearful night is this!
There's two or three of us have seen strange sights.

Cassius Am I not stayed for? Tell me.

Cinna   Yes, you are.
O Cassius, if you could   140
But win the noble Brutus to our party —

Cassius Be you content. Good Cinna, take this paper
And look you lay it in the praetor's chair,
Where Brutus may but find it. And throw this
In at his window. Set this up with wax   145
Upon old Brutus' statue. All this done,
Repair to Pompey's Porch, where you shall find us.
Is Decius Brutus and Trebonius there?

Cinna All but Metellus Cimber, and he's gone
To seek you at your house. Well, I will hie   150
And so bestow the papers as you bade me.

Cassius That done, repair to Pompey's Theatre.

[*Exit* CINNA.]
Come, Casca, you and I will yet ere day
See Brutus at his house. Three parts of him
Is ours already, and the man entire   155
Upon the next encounter yields him ours.

Casca O, he sits high in all the people's hearts;
And that which would appear offence in us,
His countenance, like richest alchemy,
Will change to virtue and to worthiness.   160

Cassius Him and his worth and our great need of
him
You have right well conceited. Let us go,
For it is after midnight; and ere day
We will awake him and be sure of him. [*Exeunt.*]

135–6. *incorporate / To:* part of.

137. *glad on't:* Cinna's answer is to the news that Casca is one of the conspirators. Cassius repeats his question.

143. *praetor:* magistrate; an office at this time held by Brutus.

146. *old Brutus' statue:* see I.2.159.

150. *hie:* hurry.

159. *His countenance:* (1) his face, (2) his approval.

alchemy: the alchemists tried to change base metals into gold. Whenever Shakespeare uses the word it is associated with the failure, or falsity of this pseudo-science. Thus its effect in Casca's speech is unconsciously ironic. Although Casca cannot know it yet, the addition of Brutus does not change the conspirator's plot "to virtue and to worthiness."

162. *well conceited:* both correctly conceived and aptly expressed.

COMMENTARY

One month has passed since the end of the last scene. It is now the eve of the Ides of March, and a storm, unlike any ever seen, is raging in Rome. Fire drops from the skies, bodies spontaneously combust, lions roam the capitol, ghostly women walk the streets, and the night owl was seen shrieking in the daylight. Casca enters with his sword drawn and his fright is apparent as he encounters Cicero.

Second only to Caesar, Marcus Tullius Cicero, born in 106 B.C., was the most important man in Rome. Highly educated in Greece, Cicero became Rome's most prominent lawyer and orator. Despite his excellent reputation and acclaimed achievements, Cicero was feared by Julius Caesar who made things so difficult for Cicero in Rome that he was driven out of Italy in 59 B.C. Cicero joined forces with Pompey, but when it became clear that Pompey was going to be defeated, Cicero pleaded for mercy from Caesar, and as was his habit, Caesar pardoned Cicero. Cicero returned to Rome and to the Senate, where he remained publicly neutral to Caesar's reforms of the government.

Unlike our modern theatres, with computerized special effects and state of the art sound systems, the Elizabethan theatre relied mainly on words to paint the scenery and suggest the sounds of thunder and lightning. Elizabethan stagehands were not without a certain amount of clever inventiveness, however, and some sound and lighting effects could be created. For example, beating drums or rolling large round bullets backstage often produced the sound of thunder. The effect of lightning could be contrived by blowing rosin through a candle flame to create a bright flash of fire.

Shakespeare, like many other writers, uses storms to create a mood of darkness and foreboding, but here he takes the image one step further. The turmoil of the heavens is directly representative of the turmoil present in the state and in the minds of men. The raging storm, coupled with the eerie sights that Casca describes, are signs of disharmony in heaven and on earth. Signs and omens, by their very nature, are meant to be interpreted and the misinterpretation and manipulation of signs and omens become important thematic issues in *Julius Caesar*. The ambiguities present in the people and the events of this play are underscored as Cicero points out to Casca, "men may construe things after their fashion / Clean from the purpose of the things themselves." Casca, dismayed by the storm, suggests that there is either civil strife in heaven or the gods are angry at the deeds of men. He fears that the gods do not approve of what the conspirators are planning to do and feels that the omens bode only evil and misfortune. Cassius, on the other hand, feels that the storm and the omens are signs that the gods are angry at Caesar's tyranny.

In the face of the irate heavens, Casca loses his use of sarcastic prose and begins to speak in blank verse. The imagery of the storm as Casca describes it in lines 3–11 is infused with metaphorical references to Caesar. He speaks of the earth that "shakes like a thing infirm" just as the epileptic Caesar shook when he had to refuse the crown. Casca speaks of the "ambitious ocean" that will "swell and rage and foam." The picture that he draws is reminiscent of an ambitious tyrant, whose ego is swelled by his power, one who rages at not getting his way and ends by foaming at the mouth in an epileptic fit.

After Cassius admonishes Casca in particular and Rome in general for being weak and "womanish," Casca makes the announcement that the Senate plans to make Caesar king in the assembly the following day. Historically, Caesar had called the senate into an emergency session set to meet on March 15. Caesar might have instigated the session to have the Senate approve a declaration of war against the Parthenians. However, some historians speculate that he was to be made King of the Provinces with the anticipation that, as the outlying cities of Italy accepted Caesar as King, the city of Rome would quickly follow. If the conspirators intend to stop Caesar before he is crowned, they must do it tomorrow before the Senate has the opportunity to convene.

Cassius is disgusted by what he interprets as the apathy of the Roman people, whom he sees as mere sheep that would blindly follow their leader into whatever dangers he might lead them. Metaphorically, Cassius sees the commoners as trash and rubbish. Recalling the image of fire, they become the "base matter" or fuel that will "illuminate" or inflame the ego of the "vile" Caesar.

Between Cassius' interpretation of the storm as the gods raging against Caesar's tyranny and the fact that Caesar may be crowned king the following day, Casca is persuaded to join forces with Cassius. Lucius Cornelius Cinna, whose father had been Caesar's first father-in-law, enters the scene, and the list of the conspirators grows to include Cinna, Decius Brutus, and Gaius Trebonius. Both Decius Brutus and Trebonius were considered to be close friends of Julius Caesar. Caesar had appointed Trebonius chief magistrate of Rome, an influential and honorable position. Caesar so loved Decius Brutus that he had named him as one of his heirs, if no other member of his family survived him.

All of these men who are now plotting to eliminate Caesar were indebted to him for either pardoning them as prisoners of war and/or placing them in high positions of honor. The meaning of friendship is an issue in this play and here we see Caesar's so-called friends plot against him. They will use their position as Caesar's friends to get close enough to Caesar to kill him.

Cassius, having forged several letters meant to influence Brutus' decision to join the conspiracy, instructs Cinna to place the letters where Brutus will be sure to find them. Cinna exits to leave the letters in Brutus' office, to place one on the statue of Brutus' ancestor and throw others into Brutus' window. Just as the conspirators plan to destroy their friend Caesar, they plot

Pompeii's Theatre (or "Pompey's porch," as referred to by Cassius). Michelle Jones/Ancient Art & Architecture Collection Ltd.

against their friend Brutus as well. Using dishonest means to persuade Brutus to join in the group shows a blatant disregard for the true meaning of friendship. Brutus is not being wooed to join the conspiracy because of a sense of brotherhood coming from these other men. He is being used because the common people see him as "noble." His presence in the conspiracy will make the vile and immoral act of murder appear to be an acceptable deed teeming with "virtue" and "worthiness."

Notes

Notes

Portia *O constancy, be strong upon my side,*
Set a huge mountain 'tween my heart and tongue!
I have a man's mind, but a woman's might.
How hard it is for women to keep counsel!

Act II, Scene 1

Alone in his garden, Brutus contemplates the implications of joining Cassius and the other conspirators. Based on the possibility of what might happen if Caesar gains more power, Brutus agrees that Caesar must die. The conspirators, along with Cassius, visit Brutus and the men make their plans for the following day. After the men leave, Brutus' wife Portia asks to know what is troubling her husband. She has gashed her leg in an effort to prove to Brutus that she is strong enough to endure anything he may tell her. As he is preparing to tell her, there is a knock at the door and Brutus promises Portia he will reveal all his secrets to her as soon as possible.

ACT II, SCENE 1
Brutus' orchard.

[*Enter* BRUTUS.]

Brutus What, Lucius, ho!
  I cannot by the progress of the stars
  Give guess how near to day. Lucius I say!
  I would it were my fault to sleep so soundly.
  When, Lucius, when? Awake, I say! What, Lucius!   5

[*Enter* LUCIUS.]

Lucius Called you, my lord?

Brutus Get me a taper in my study, Lucius.
  When it is lighted, come and call me here.

Lucius I will, my lord. [*Exit.*]

Brutus It must be by his death; and for my part,   10
  I know no personal cause to spurn at him,
  But for the general. He would be crowned.
  How that might change his nature, there the question.
  It is the bright day that brings forth the adder,
  And that craves wary walking. Crown him that   15
  And then I grant we put a sting in him
  That at his will he may do danger with.
  Th' abuse of greatness is, when it disjoins
  Remorse from power. And to speak truth of Caesar
  I have not known when his affections swayed   20
  More than his reason. But 'tis common proof

NOTES

5.   *When . . . when . . . What:* exclamations of impatience.

7.   *taper:* candle.

11. *spurn:* kick at/be scornful to.

12. *the general:* general reasons in the interest of the public good.

14–15. *It . . . walking:* i.e., the sunshine brings out the adder and makes careful walking necessary.

15. *Crown him that:* Brutus hesitates at the distasteful word king.

19. *Remorse:* the word meant mercy or humanity in a general sense to the Elizabethans.

20. *affections swayed:* passions ruled.

21. *common proof:* common experience.

That lowliness is young ambition's ladder,
Whereto the climber upward turns his face;
But when lie once attains the upmost round,
He then unto the ladder turns his back,   25
Looks in the clouds, scorning the base degrees
By which he did ascend. So Caesar may.
Then lest he may, prevent. And since the quarrel
Will bear no colour for the thing he is,
Fashion it thus: that what he is, augmented,   30
Would run to these and these extremities;
And therefore think him as a serpent's egg,
Which, hatched, would as his kind grow mischievous
And kill him in the shell.

[*Enter* LUCIUS.]

Lucius The taper burneth in your closet, sir.   35
Searching the window for a flint, I found
This paper, thus sealed tip; and I am sure
It did not lie there when I went to bed.

[*Gives him a letter.*]

Brutus Get you to bed again; it is not day.
Is not to-morrow, boy, the ides of March?   40

Lucius I know not, sir.

Brutus Look in the calendar and bring me word.

Lucius I will, sir.

Brutus These exhalations, whizzing in the air,
Gives so much light that I may read by them.   45

[*Opens the letter and reads.*]
'Brutus, thou sleep'st. Awake and see thyself!
Shall Rome, &c. Speak, strike, redress!'
Brutus, thou sleep'st. Awake!
Such instigations have been often dropped
Where I have took them up.   50
'Shall Rome, &c.' Thus must I piece it out:
Shall Rome stand under one man's awe? What, Rome?
My ancestors did from the streets of Rome
The Tarquin drive when he was called a king.
'Speak, strike, redress!' Am I entreated   55

---

22. *lowliness:* false humility.

26. *base degrees:* both (1) rungs of the ladder, and (2) lower ranks.

29. *colour:* excuse.

     he: it.

30. *Fashion:* shape, change the form of.

31. *extremities:* extremes of power/tyranny

33. *his kind:* his nature.

35. *closet:* study.

44. *exhalations:* meteors. Brutus recalls to the audience that the storm continues; it underlines the tension throughout the scene. See commentary at I.3.

51. *piece it out:* fill it in.

To speak and strike? O Rome, I make thee promise,
If the redress will follow, thou receivest
Thy full petition at the hand of Brutus.

[*Enter* LUCIUS.]

Lucius Sir, March is wasted fifteen days.

[*Knock within.*]

Brutus 'Tis good. Go to the gate; somebody knocks.   60

[*Exit* LUCIUS.]
Since Cassius first did whet me against Caesar,
I have not slept.
Between the acting of a dreadful thing
And the first motion, all the interim is
Like a phantasma or a hideous dream.   65
The genius and the mortal instruments
Are then in council, and the state of man,
Like to a little kingdom, suffers then
The nature of an insurrection.

[*Enter* LUCIUS.]

Lucius Sir, 'tis your brother Cassius at the door,   70
Who doth desire to see you.

Brutus   Is he alone?

Lucius No, sir. There are moe with him.

Brutus   Do you know them?

Lucius No, Sir. Their hats are plucked about
their ears
And half their faces buried in their cloaks,
That by no means I may discover them   75
By any mark of favour.

Brutus   Let 'em enter. [*Exit* LUCIUS.]
They are the faction. O conspiracy,
Sham'st thou to show thy dangerous brow by night,
When evils are most free? O, then by day
Where wilt thou find a cavern dark enough   80
To mask thy monstrous visage? Seek none,
    conspiracy.

58. *thy full petition:* all you ask.

S.D. *within:* i.e., offstage.

61. *whet:* sharpened like a knife.

65. *phantasma:* horrible illusion.

66. *genius . . . instruments:* spirit and faculties.

72. *moe:* more.

76. *favour:* feature.

Hide it in smiles and affability:
For if thou put thy native semblance on,
Not Erebus itself were dim enough
To hide thee from prevention.   85

[*Enter the conspirators,* CASSIUS, CASCA, DECIUS,
    CINNA, METELLUS CIMBER, *and* TREBONIUS.]

Cassius I think we are too bold upon your rest.
    Good morrow, Brutus. Do we trouble you?

Brutus I have been up this hour, awake all night.
    Know I these men that come along with you?

Cassius Yes, every man of them; and no man here   90
    But honours you; and every one doth wish
    You had but that opinion of yourself
    Which every noble Roman bears of you.
    This is Trebonius.

Brutus   He is welcome hither.

Cassius This, Decius Brutus.   95

Brutus   He is welcome too.

Cassius This, Casca; this, Cinna; and this Metellus
    Cimber.

Brutus They are all welcome.
    What watchful cares do interpose themselves
    Betwixt your eyes and night?

Cassius Shall I entreat a word? [*They whisper.*]   100

Decius Here lies the east. Doth not the day break
    here?

Casca No.

Cinna O, pardon sir, it doth; and yon grey lines
    That fret the clouds are messengers of day.

Casca You shall confess that you are both deceived.   105
    Here, as I point my sword, the sun arises,
    Which is a great way growing on the south,
    Weighing the youthful season of the year.
    Some two months hence, up higher toward the north
    He first presents his fire; and the high east   110

83.   *native semblance:* natural appearance. Some editors read "path" (walk) for "put" in this line.

84.   *Erebus:* in classical mythology, a region of darkness between Earth and Hades.

85.   *prevention:* being forestalled.

98.   *watchful cares:* cares that keep one awake.

107. *growing on:* toward.

Stands as the Capitol, directly here.

Brutus Give me your hands all over, one by one.

Cassius And let us swear our resolution.

Brutus No, not an oath. If not the face of men,
The sufferance of our souls, the time's abuse —   115
If these be motives weak, break off betimes,
And every man hence to his idle bed.
So let high-sighted tyranny rage on
Till each man drop by lottery. But if these
(As I am sure they do) bear fire enough   120
To kindle cowards and to steel with valour
The melting spirits of women, then, countrymen,
What need we any spur but our own cause
To prick us to redress? what other bond
Than secret Romans that have spoke the word   125
And will not palter? and what other oath
Than honesty to honesty engaged
That this shall be, or we will fall for it?
Swear priests and cowards and men cautelous,
Old feeble carrions and such suffering souls   130
That welcome wrongs; unto bad causes swear
Such creatures as men doubt; but do not stain
The even virtue of our enterprise,
Nor th' insuppressive mettle of our spirits,
To think that or our cause or our performance   135
Did need an oath; when every drop of blood
That every Roman bears, and nobly bears,
Is guilty of a several bastardy
If he do break the smallest particle
Of any promise that hath passed from him.   140

Cassius But what of Cicero? Shall we sound him?
I think he will stand very strong with us.

Casca Let us not leave him out.

Cinna   No, by no means.

Metellus O, let us have him! for his silver hairs
Will purchase us a good opinion   145
And buy men's voices to commend our deeds.

114–6. "if the misery in men's faces, the suffering in their souls, the evils of the time are not strong enough motives." (J. H. Walter)

116. *betimes:* at once.

118. *high-sighted:* ambitious.

119. *by lottery:* by chance.
if these: i.e., these motives.

124. *prick:* spur.

126. *palter:* quibble or deceive.

129. *cautelous:* crafty.

130. *carrions:* living carcasses.

134. *insuppressive:* unsuppressable; indomitable.

138. *several bastardy:* i.e., a separate act, showing it not to be true Roman blood.

145. *opinion:* reputation.

It shall be said his judgment ruled our hands.
Our youths and wildness shall no whit appear,
But all be buried in his gravity.

Brutus O, name him not! Let us not break with   150
    him;
For he will never follow anything
That other men begin.

Cassius   Then leave him out.

Casca Indeed he is not fit.

Decius Shall no man else be touched but only
    Caesar?

Cassius Decius, well urged. I think it is not meet   155
Mark Antony, so well beloved of Caesar,
Should outlive Caesar. We shall find of him
A shrewd contriver; and you know, his means,
If he improve them, may well stretch so far
As to annoy us all; which, to prevent,   160
Let Antony and Caesar fall together.

Brutus Our course will seem too bloody, Caius
    Cassius,
To cut the head off and then hack the limbs,
Like wrath in death and envy afterwards;
For Antony is but a limb of Caesar.   165
Let's be sacrificers, but not butchers, Caius.
We all stand up against the spirit of Caesar,
And in the spirit of men there is no blood.
O that we then could come by Caesar's spirit
And not dismember Caesar! But, alas,   170
Caesar must bleed for it! And, gentle friends,
Let's kill him boldly, but not wrathfully;
Let's carve him as a dish fit for the gods,
Not hew him as a carcass fit for hounds.
And let our hearts, as subtle masters do,   175
Stir up their servants to an act of rage
And after seem to chide 'em. This shall make
Our purpose necessary, and not envious;
Which so appearing to the common eyes,
We shall be called purgers, not murderers.   180

---

148.   *no whit:* none at all.

149.   *gravity:* authority.

150.   *break with:* break our news to, discuss.

158.   *means:* powers.

164.   *envy:* malice.

175–7.   *And . . . 'em:* i.e., let our hearts excite our hands to an act of violence, and afterwards rebuke them.

178.   *envious:* malicious.

180.   *purgers:* healers who heal by letting blood.

And for Mark Antony, think not of him;
For he can do no more than Caesar's arm
When Caesar's head is off.

Cassius   Yet I fear him;
For in the ingrafted love he bears to Caesar —

Brutus Alas, good Cassius, do not think of him!   185
If he love Caesar, all that he can do
Is to himself — take thought, and die for Caesar.
And that were much he should; for he is given
To sports, to wildness, and much company.

Trebonius There is no fear in him. Let him not die;   190
For he will live, and laugh at this hereafter.

[*Clock strikes.*]

Brutus Peace! Count the clock.

Cassius   The clock hath stricken three.

Trebonius 'Tis time to part.

Cassius   But it is doubtful yet
Whether Caesar will come forth to-day or no;
For he is superstitious grown of late,   195
Quite from the main opinion he held once
Of fantasy, of dreams, and ceremonies.
It may be these apparent prodigies,
The unaccustomed terror of this night,
And the persuasion of his augurers   200
May hold him from the Capitol to-day.

Decius Never fear that. If he be so resolved,
I can o'ersway him; for he loves to hear
That unicorns may be betrayed with trees
And bears with glasses, elephants with holes,   205
Lions with toils, and men with flatterers;
But when I tell him he hates flatterers,
He says he does, being then most flattered.
Let me work;
For I can give his humour the true bent   210
And I will bring him to the Capitol.

Cassius Nay, we will all of us be there to fetch him.

184.   *ingrafted:* deep-rooted.

188.   *And . . . should:* i.e., that is too much to expect of him.

190.   *no fear:* nothing to fear.

196.   *from the main:* as opposed to the strong.

197.   *ceremonies:* portents, omens.

198.   *apparent prodigies:* wonders that have appeared.

200.   *augurers:* priests who interpreted omens.

204.   *betrayed with trees:* i.e., tricked into running their horns into trees, and thus easily captured.

205.   *glasses:* mirrors, in which they think they see other bears.

       holes: pits as traps.

206.   *toils:* snares.

       flatterers: i.e., flatterers are to men as the various snares are to animals.

210.   *humour bent:* i.e., I can guide his mood.

212.   *fetch:* escort.

Brutus By the eighth hour. Is that the uttermost?

Cinna Be that the uttermost, and fail not then.

Metellus Caius Ligarius doth bear Caesar hard,   215
Who rated him for speaking well of Pompey.
I wonder none of you have thought of him.

Brutus Now, good Metellius, go along by him.
He loves me well, and I have given him reasons
Send him but hither, and I'll fashion him.   220

Cassius The morning comes upon 's. We'll leave
       you, Brutus.
And, friends, disperse yourselves; but all remember
What we have said and show yourselves true Romans.

Brutus Good gentlemen, look fresh and merrily.
Let not our looks put on our purposes,   225
But bear it as our Roman actors do,
With untired spirits and formal constancy.
And so good morrow to you every one.
[*Exeunt all except* BRUTUS.]
Boy! Lucius! Fast asleep? It is no matter.
Enjoy the honey-heavy due of slumber.   230
Thou has no figures nor no fantasies
Which busy care draws in the brains of men;
Therefore thou sleep'st so sound.

[*Enter* PORTIA.]

Portia   Brutus, my lord.

Brutus Portia! What mean you? Wherefore rise
       you now?
It is not for your health thus to commit   235
Your weak condition to the raw cold morning.

Portia Nor for yours neither. Y' have ungently,
       Brutus,
Stole from my bed. And yesternight at supper
You suddenly arose and walked about,
Musing and sighing with your arms across: 240
And when I asked you what the matter was,
You stared upon me with ungentle looks.
I urged you further; then you scratched your head

213.   *uttermost:* latest.

215.   *bear Caesar hard:* bear a grudge against Caesar.

216.   *rated:* upbraided.

218.   *by him:* to his house.

220.   *fashion:* shape (to our purpose).

225.   *put on:* reveal.

227.   *formal constancy:* steadfast self-possession.

230.   *honey-heavy due:* sweet dreams.

231.   *figures:* i.e., the mind; fantasies.

235.   *commit:* expose.

236.   *condition:* constitution.

237.   *ungently:* discourteously.

240.   *across:* folded across your chest, held by the Elizabethans to be a sign of melancholy.

And too impatiently stamped with your foot.
Yet I insisted; yet you answered not,   245
But with an angry wafter of your hand

246.   *wafter:* wave.

Gave sign for me to leave you. So I did,
Fearing to strengthen that impatience
Which seemed too much enkindled, and withal
Hoping it was but an effect of humor,   250

250.   *humor:* mood; here, ill-humor.

Which sometime hath his hour with every man.
It will not let you cat nor talk nor sleep,
And could it work so much upon your shape

253.   *shape:* physical appearance.

As it hath much prevailed on your condition,

254.   *condition:* state of mind.

I should not know you Brutus. Dear my lord,   255
Make me acquainted with your cause of grief.

Brutus I am not well in health, and that is all.

Portia Brutus is wise and, were he not in health,
He would embrace the means to come by it.

Brutus Why so I do. Good Portia, go to bed.   260

Portia Is Brutus sick, and is it physical

261.   *physical:* healthy.

To walk unbraced and suck up the humours

262.   *unbraced:* with the doublet open.

Of the dank morning? What, is Brutus sick,

       humours: mists.

And will he steal out of his wholesome bed
To dare the vile contagion of the night,   265

265.   *To . . . night:* Night air was thought to be unhealthy.
       There is also a reference here, although Portia does
       not know it, to the night, or darkness, of conspiracy.

And tempt the rheumy and unpurged air,

266.   *rheumy:* moist.

To add unto his sickness? No, my Brutus.

       unpurged: not yet purified by the sun.

You have some sick offence within your mind,
Which by the right and virtue of my place

268.   *sick offence:* harmful illness.

I ought to know of; and upon my knees   270
I charm you, by my once commended beauty,

271.   *charm:* means both (1) persuade and (2) charm with
       her beauty.

By all your vows of love; and that great vow
Which did incorporate and make us one,

273.   *incorporate:* join together.

That you unfold to me, your self, your half,

274.   *half:* i.e., other half.

Why you are heavy — and what men to-night   275
Have had resort to you; for here have been
Some six or seven, who did hide their faces
Even from darkness.

Brutus   Kneel not, gentle Portia.

Portia I should not need if you were gentle Brutus.

Within the bond of marriage, tell me, Brutus,   280
It is excepted I should know no secrets
That appertain to you? Am I your self
But, as it were, in sort or limitation?
To keep with you at meals, comfort your bed,
And talk to you sometimes? Dwell I but in the   285
     suburbs
Of your good pleasure? If it be no more,
Portia is Brutus' harlot, not his wife.

Brutus You are my true and honourable wife,
As dear to me as are the ruddy drops
That visit my sad heart.   290

Portia If this were true, then should I know this
     secret.
I grant I am a woman; but withal
A woman that Lord Brutus took to wife.
I grant I am a woman; but withal
A woman well-reputed, Cato's daughter.   295
Think you I am no stronger than my sex,
Being so fathered and so husbanded?
Tell me your counsels; I will not disclose 'em.
I have made strong proof of my constancy,
Giving myself a voluntary wound   300
Here, in the thigh. Can I bear that with patience,
And not my husband's secrets?

Brutus   O ye gods,
Render me worthy of this noble wife!

[*Knocking within.*]
Hark! hark! One knocks. Portia, go in awhile,
And by and by thy bosom shall partake   305
The secrets of my heart.
All my engagements I will construe thee,
And all the charactery of my sad brows.
Leave me with haste. [*Exit* PORTIA.]
                    Lucius, who's that knocks?

[*Enter* LUCIUS *and* CAIUS LIGARIUS.]

Lucius Here is a sick man that would speak with   310
     you.

280–3. *bond, excepted, sort or limitation:* these are all Elizabethan legal terms. The meaning is, is it part of the marriage contract that I should not know your secrets? Am I only a limited part of you?

285. *suburbs:* London suburbs, notorious for prostitution. This idea introduces "harlot" in line 287.

298. *counsels:* secret plans.

299. *proof of constancy:* test of endurance.

307. *engagements:* commitments.

308. *charactery:* what is written upon, i.e., the meaning.

Brutus Caius Ligarius, that Metellus spake of.
  Boy stand aside. Caius Ligarius, how?

Caius Vouchsafe good morrow from a feeble tongue.

Brutus O, what a time have you chose out, brave
    Caius,
  To wear a kerchief! Would you were not sick!   315

Caius I am not sick if Brutus have in hand
  Any exploit worthy the name of honour.

Brutus Such an exploit have I in hand, Ligarius,
  Had you a healthful ear to hear of it.

Cassius By all the gods that Romans bow before,   320
  I here discard my sickness. [*Throws off his kerchief.*]
      Soul of Rome,
  Brave son derived from honourable loins,
  Thou like an exorcist hast conjured up
  My mortified spirit. Now bid me run,
  And I will strive with things impossible;   325
  Yea, get the better of them. What's to do?

Brutus A piece of work that will make sick men
      whole.

Caius But are not some whole that we must make
      sick?

Brutus That must we also. What it is, my Caius,
  I shall unfold to thee as we are going,   330
  To whom it must be done.

Caius   Set on your foot,
  And with a heart new-fired I follow you,
  To do I know not what; but it sufficeth
  That Brutus leads me on. [*Thunder.*]   335

Brutus Follow me then. [*Exeunt.*]

312. *how?:* exclamation of surprise.

315. *wear a kerchief:* i.e., wear some sort of bandage, be ill.

322. *derived . . . loins:* of honorable descent.

323. *exorcist:* one who frees others from evil spirits.

324. *mortified:* as though dead.

327. *whole:* well. Brutus extends Ligarius' idea of recovery from sickness to the conspiracy.

328. *make sick:* euphemisim for kill.

331. *to whom:* i.e., and to whom.

COMMENTARY

Scholars speculate that *Hamlet* was written immediately after Shakespeare finished *Julius Caesar*. If that is the case, it would seem quite likely that the soul-searching Brutus became the prototype for the character of Hamlet. Just as Hamlet endlessly questions and analyzes his actions, Brutus, in Act II, Scene 1, contemplates the ramifications of joining the conspiracy against Julius Caesar.

Scene 1 takes place in Brutus' garden, usually a place of quiet tranquility where a man may commune with nature. Tonight, however, a storm has raged in Rome and Brutus' private domain is, like the rest of nature, in terrible turmoil. As in the previous scene, the unnatural disharmony of the universe is symbolic of the dissonance of the state and representative of the discord in Brutus' soul. There is such chaos in the cosmos that even time is out of joint: "I cannot by the progress of the stars / Give guess how near to day."

Brutus is not only unable to determine the time of day; he also has trouble remembering what day of the month it is. In the 1623 Folio version of the play, line 40 reads, "Is not tomorrow the first of March?" Many editors change the line to read "the Ides of March" but it is possible that both Shakespeare and his audience would have understood Brutus' confusion about time. On one level, Brutus' inability to determine the time and date would suggest that he is equally unable to understand the times in which he is living. The people of Rome are happy and content with their leader and Brutus, like Cassius in the previous scene, will refuse to see that. His confusion with time could also be a direct reference to a major political issue occurring in England and throughout Europe at the time *Julius Caesar* was written.

Julius Caesar is credited with creating the Julian calendar and Plutarch suggests that many of Caesar's detractors cited the new calendar as evidence against him. They claimed his implementation of the calendar was proof of his tyrannical tendencies and that his manipulation of time was an interference with the true course of nature. By the year 1582, the Julian calendar had drifted ten days out of phase and Pope Gregory decreed the reform of the existing calendar. The Catholic followers of the Pope adopted the new calendar whereas the Protestants rejected it. The issue of calendar reform became an intense political struggle in Europe. By 1598, the year before Shakespeare is thought to have written *Julius Caesar*, there were five weeks separating the celebrations of the Catholic Easter and the Protestant Easter. Many of the English Protestants, like the Romans before them, felt that being forced by Queen Elizabeth to maintain the Julian calendar was tyrannical and an interference with the true course of nature.

Brutus' envy of his servant Lucius' ability to sleep soundly suggests that his mind has been recently troubled and it is worry over Caesar's power that prevents him from finding rest. In referring to the lean and hungry Cassius in the previous act, Caesar intimates that men who cannot sleep at night are dangerous and now the sleepless Brutus will indeed become a danger to Julius Caesar. In his nocturnal ruminations, Brutus has begun to convince himself that Caesar must die.

Brutus' interior debate and the ensuing verdict that Caesar must be assassinated illustrates some of the major flaws in Brutus' character. He sees himself as a noble man with a strong sense of morality and works hard to maintain that image with the public. In this soliloquy, however, the audience sees a man who can convince himself that murder is an appropriate answer based solely on conjecture. Brutus merely speculates that Caesar may become too powerful and in anticipation of what that power may do, he makes his decision to support the actions of the conspiracy. History consistently demonstrates that power can corrupt, but if the populace decided to eliminate all politicians based on the possibility that they may become power-hungry, there would be no leaders left. Brutus' decision to join in the plot to murder Caesar is based on fallacious logic and shows him as a man who considers his knowledge of human nature so great that he is capable of seeing into the future. By assuming to play god, he can prevent what he, in his own infinite wisdom, sees as harmful to Rome. In this light, is Brutus any different than Caesar? Caesar, based on his reforms in Italy, is judged harshly for wanting Rome to conform to his worldview and here Brutus behaves just like the man he will kill. In doing so, he forces the world to conform to his personal vision of it. Brutus is so concerned with his sense of self that he does not recognize his irrational logic and inability to reason; this fault will undermine the conspiracy and create havoc in the Rome he professes to love so dearly.

In addition to Brutus' skewed logic, his susceptible vanity and inordinate pride are also highlighted in this scene. Lucius, finding one of the forged letters that has been thrown into Brutus' window, brings the note to Brutus who fails to recognize it as a forgery. Instead, he views the note as a public affirmation of his recent decision to eliminate Caesar. His pride at being an ancestor of the man who vanquished the Tarquin King spurs him to fill in the blanks of the forged note with his own version of what the people want. He himself will vanquish a King and take his place among the great heroes of Rome.

Brutus is completely aware of the hideous quality of the conspiracy as he personifies it as a monster in lines 78–85. He may delude himself when searching his soul for the motives for killing Caesar, but he knows without a doubt that the act is an evil thing that should be hidden away. Brutus is nothing if not a consummate politician and he is cognizant of the fact that it is often necessary in politics to mask a monster with "smiles and affability."

Shakespeare's reference to Erebus in this passage is packed with meaning and is an interesting segue into the next section of the text. According to Greek mythology, Erebus, the dark underground passage to Hell, was born of Chaos. Chaos was the primordial void that existed before order was created in the universe and from which all things, including the gods, proceeded. Immediately following the reference, Cassius and the other conspirators emerge from the dark, chaotic night and take their places in the dark and chaotic history of Rome that will follow the death of Caesar.

Cassius, always a man focused on his mission, greets Brutus with words of flattery and the two men move to one side, conversing in whispers while the other conspirators take center stage. In this portion of the scene, Shakespeare again depicts the inability of men to tell the time of day. Not only does the writer draw attention to the incompetence of these men to judge the times they live in but he also shows them as an unorganized and contradictory group who cannot agree on where the sun rises, much less on issues of vast political importance.

Brutus, as the newest official member of the conspiracy, begins his association with this group of bumbling and confused men with a few blunders of his own. Cassius suggests that the conspirators swear an oath, which Brutus quickly vetoes. Although Brutus knows murder is a dishonorable act, he must find a way to "fashion" it into something noble and virtuous and to swear an oath, would give the conspiracy an appearance of secrecy and exclusivity. An oath would also give way to the possibilities of lies and betrayals of that oath, and "appearance," important to a politician, is vital to Brutus' personal sense of honor to give this endeavor the look of honesty and lofty ideals.

The next issue to be broached is the possible addition of Cicero to the list of conspirators. As revealed earlier, Cicero was an excellent and coercive speaker. He knew the law and, as seen in contrast to Casca in the storm scene, Cicero is calm and collected under pressure. He would be an invaluable addition to the conspiracy but again, Brutus says no. This time he cites the excuse that Cicero "will never follow anything / That other men begin." Brutus is intimidated by Cicero's tendency to be a leader rather than a follower. If Cicero took the lead in this enterprise, who would then be noted by history as the man who freed Rome from its tyrant king? Cassius, in his effort to keep Brutus content and part of the conspiracy, concedes to him again.

Decius then asks if anyone other than Caesar should "be touched." Cassius quickly responds that it would benefit their plans if "Antony and Caesar fall together." Where Brutus is a political idealist, Cassius is a political realist. Cassius understands the workings of human nature and is a much better judge of character than Brutus. He knows that Antony is not only a loyal friend to Caesar but also a fine soldier and would be in a solid position to mount an attack against the conspiracy. Brutus, on the other hand, sees only Antony's weaknesses: "he is given / To sports, to wildness, and much company." Shakespeare, again using the image of the body politic, has Brutus compare Antony to merely a limb of the body that will wither and die when the head, Caesar, is severed. In underestimating Antony's strengths, Brutus continues on the course that will doom the conspiracy to failure.

Brutus' reticence to kill Antony along with Caesar is at first glance a noble one, but a closer look at his motives reveals a clever politician attempting to do a little spin-doctoring. Just as Caesar attempted at the beginning of the play to make the Feast of the Lupercal, a religious ceremony, into a political one, Brutus now desires to make a political act into something religious. If Brutus can succeed at making an act of cold-blooded murder done to advance the personal ambitions of a small group of men into something that is perceived as sacred, he will have achieved two things. Personally, he will be able to relieve his own conscience by rationalizing an immoral act as something moral. In addition, if the act appears as a religious sacrifice, the "common eyes" of the people of Rome will believe that what the conspirators have done was "necessary, and not envious." Brutus, like every good politician, is concerned with how his actions are interpreted by the general populace and seeks to manipulate situations to win their approval.

As the final plans are drawn for Caesar's assassination, the clock strikes three. In the majority of editions of *Julius Caesar*, the striking clock is often identified as an anachronism. There were no mechanical clocks in the Rome of Julius Caesar, but, as opposed to being a mistake by the writer, the striking clock could serve as another reminder that the time or the times they are living in are out of sync. Also, the fact that Brutus asks the conspirators to "Count the clock" may be Shakespeare's way of underscoring the number three as a number identified with betrayal. The majority of Elizabethans watching the play would perhaps associate the number three with the number of times that Peter betrayed Jesus and also with the time, according to the Bible, that Jesus died upon the cross.

The men prepare to leave and Cassius expresses his concern that, because Caesar has recently become superstitious, he might choose not go to the Capitol. Decius assures the others that he will be able to convince Caesar to go to the Capitol no matter what mood he may be in and volunteers to escort him to the Capitol himself. Cassius insists that everyone should meet Caesar and they all should accompany him to the Capitol. The plot is set, the hour agreed upon and Brutus bids farewell to the conspirators with an admonishment to conceal their purpose and, like actors, put on the mask of normalcy.

Up until this point in the play, only the public Brutus has been seen. With the entrance of his wife, Portia, the reader has the opportunity to witness the private Brutus. He is a very different man within the confines of his own home. He is gentle with his servant, Lucius, and seems genuinely worried about Portia when she enters the scene, expressing concern that she is exposing herself to the "raw cold morning." Portia paints a portrait of what her husband has recently become and by doing so illustrates for the audience what the private Brutus was before becoming involved in the plot against Caesar. Brutus shows evidence of being a man who has the capacity to feel deeply about people and their situations but unfortunately chooses to deny those feelings in public in an effort to maintain his honorable and stoic image.

Portia was Brutus' first cousin as well as his second wife. At the time the play takes place, they had been married for about two years. She was the daughter of Marcus Porcuis Cato or "Cato the Younger," a leader in Pompey's army who fought against Caesar in Africa. Known for his steadfast virtue and adherence to his principles, Cato committed suicide rather than surrender to Caesar's army. Portia herself is a strong woman, proud of her lineage, and not afraid to confront her husband or take a stand for equality in her marriage. She confronts Brutus, demanding to know why he is so troubled, and she does not allow him to cover his activities with evasive stories about ill health. Appealing to Brutus' own sense of honor, she questions if he is dishonoring her by not sharing his secrets with her. Brutus, in one of his most sincere and heartfelt responses, replies that she is his "true and honourable wife, / As dear to me as are the ruddy drops / That visit my sad heart."

Portia reminds Brutus of her heritage and by association hopes to convince Brutus that she is stronger than the majority of wives. To prove her fearlessness, constancy, and equality, she shows Brutus the wound she has made on her thigh. According to Plutarch, Portia gashed herself with a razor. The gash became infected and she was quite ill, running a very high fever. It might possibly be this fever to which Brutus refers in the early part of the scene when he comments on his wife's weak health. The ability to suffer silently was highly prized as a Roman virtue and, by wounding herself, Portia seeks to prove herself constant and worthy of Brutus' trust.

Her husband is convinced of Portia's trustworthiness and promises to tell her everything as soon as possible.

The image of illness and the theme of disease runs continuously through *Julius Caesar.* Caesar's deafness, his epilepsy, and his possible inability to produce children are revealed early in Act I. Before Cassius and the other conspirators enter the scene in Act II, Brutus comments on the disease that occurs between the conception of an idea and the action that completes it. He speaks of the "genius" or soul of man being at war with his body or "mortal instruments." As the soul or spiritual nature of man battles with his mortal or base desires, the state of humanity or the body politic suffers and becomes ill. Shakespeare often compares the illness and discord in mankind to the dissonance rampant in the universe.

The scene between Brutus and Portia incorporates illness both real and speculative, and the entrance of Caius Ligarius is blatant with the images of sickness in man and in the body politic. Due to his illness, Ligarius, a senator who had originally supported Pompey but had, like the other conspirators, been pardoned by Caesar, comes late to the meeting. He tells Brutus that his illness will be cured if Brutus is involved in an "exploit worthy the name of honor." According to Brutus, this honorable exploit is, "A piece of work that will make sick men whole." Caius replies, "But are not some whole that we must make sick?" Disease is running rampant through both individuals and Rome. Caesar, the head of Rome, is suffering from overly ambitious desires for power. His illness has infected the rest of the body, or the people of Rome. Brutus cannot sleep at night and his wife fears he is ill. Portia is running a high fever from the wound she has inflicted on herself. Ligarius' health affects the conspiracy. There is no choice but to find a cure for the illness before it kills the entire body. Unfortunately, Brutus and Cassius do not effect a cure. Rather, they choose to cut off the head of the body (Caesar) in an effort to heal the body as a whole, but a body cannot live without a head, and Rome will not be cured of its ills in this way either. The body, either human or politic, must have a head. Without it, the body dies.

Brutus and Cassius have made plans to cut out the disease they have diagnosed as fatal to Rome, but their scheme seems to stop there. No discussion has ensued concerning what will happen after Caesar is dead. Who will rule Rome? Will this new regime govern the people in new ways? The conspirators are lethally shortsighted and their lack of a plan of action spells disaster for their cause, whatever that may be.

Caius Ligarius, in the final few lines of this scene, calls Brutus the "Soul of Rome." If Brutus is indeed a shining example of the conscience and spiritual nature of Rome, it is no wonder that chaos and disorder are tormenting the capitol of Italy.

Act II, Scene 2

Caesar's wife, Calpurnia, is concerned by the violent storm and the odd sightings reported throughout Rome. She has also had a dream that she fears is a warning of Caesar's death. She begs Caesar to stay home and he finally agrees. When Decius Brutus arrives to escort Caesar to the Senate, Caesar tells him he is not going. He tells Decius of Calpurnia's dream but Decius reinterprets the dream, making it an omen of good fortune. Caesar chooses to believe Decius and when the other Senators arrive, he leaves with them to go to the Capitol.

ACT II, SCENE 2
Caesar's house.

[*Thunder and lightning. Enter* JULIUS CAESAR, *in his nightgown.*]

Caesar Nor heaven nor earth have been at peace
    to-night.
Thrice hath Calpurnia in her sleep cried out
'Help ho! They murder Caesar!' Who's within?

[*Enter a* Servant.]

Servant My lord?

Caesar Go bid the priests do present sacrifice,   5
And bring me their opinions of success.

Servant I will, my lord. [*Exit.*]

[*Enter* CALPURNIA.]

Calpurnia What mean you Caesar? Think you to
    walk forth?
You shall not stir out of your house to-day.

Caesar Caesar shall forth. The things that threat-   10
    ened me
Ne'er looked but on my back. When they shall see
The face of Caesar, they are vanished.

Calpurnia Caesar, I never stood on ceremonies,
Yet now they fright me. There is one within,
Besides the things that we have heard and seen,   15
Recounts most horrid sights seen by the watch.

NOTES

S.D.   *nightgown:* dressing. gown.

1.   This is heavily ironic; Caesar's "peace" is threatened by another kind of storm.

3.   *Who's within:* i.e., which of the servants.

5.   *priests:* who conduct the auguries.
     present: immediate.

13.   *stood on ceremonies:* considered portents of any significance.

16.   *watch:* watchmen.

A lioness hath whelped in the streets,
And graves have yawned and yielded up their dead.
Fierce fiery warriors fought upon the clouds
In ranks and squadrons and right form of war,   20
Which drizzled blood upon the Capitol.
The noise of battle hurtled in the air,
Horses did neigh, and dying men did groan,
And ghosts did shriek and squeal about the streets.
O Caesar, these things are beyond all use,   25
And I do fear them!

Caesar   What can be avoided
Whose end is purposed by the mighty gods?
Yet Caesar shall go forth; for these predictions
Are to the world in general as to Caesar.

Calpurnia When beggars die there are no comets   30
        seen;
The heavens themselves blaze forth the death of
        princes.

Caesar Cowards die many times before their
        deaths;
The valiant never taste of death but once.
Of all the wonders that I yet have heard,
It seems to me most strange that men should fear,   35
Seeing that death, a necessary end,
Will come when it will come.

[*Enter a* Servant.]
                What say the augurers?

Servant They would not have you to stir forth
        to-day.
Plucking the entrails of an offering forth,
They could not find a heart within the beast.   40

Caesar The gods do this in shame of cowardice.
Caesar should be a beast without a heart
If he should stay at home to-day for fear.
No, Caesar shall not. Danger knows full well
That Caesar is more dangerous than he.   45
We are two lions littered in one day,

17.	*whelped:* given birth
20.	*right form:* battle order.
22.	*hurtled:* clashed with violence and noise.
25.	*use:* any usual experience or custom.
29.	*Are to:* apply as much to.
31.	*blaze forth:* proclaim
41.	*in shame of:* i.e., to shame the coward.
42.	*Caesar should be:* i.e., would himself be.
46.	*littered:* born.

And I the elder and more terrible,
And Caesar shall go forth.

Calpurnia　　　　　　　Alas, my lord,
Your wisdom is consumed in confidence.
Do not go forth to-day. Call it my fear 　　　50
That keeps you in the house and not your own.
We'll send Mark Antony to the Senate House,
And he shall say you are not well to-day.
Let me upon my knee prevail in this.

Caesar Mark Antony shall say I am not well, 　　　55
And for thy humour I will stay at home.

[*Enter* DECIUS.]
Here's Decius Brutus; he shall tell them so.

Decius Caesar, all hail! Good morrow, worthy
　　　Caesar;
I come to fetch you to the Senate House.

Caesar And you are come in very happy time 　　　60
To bear my greetings to the senators
And tell them that I will not come to-day.
Cannot, is false; and that I dare not, falser:
I will not come to-day. Tell them so, Decius.

Calpurnia Say he is sick. 　　　65

Caesar　　　　　　　Shall Caesar send a lie?
Have I in conquest stretched mine arm so far
To be afeard to tell greybeards the truth?
Decius, go tell them Caesar will not come.

Decius Most mighty Caesar, let me know some
　　　cause,
Lest I be laughed at when I tell them so. 　　　70

Caesar The cause is in my will: I will not come.
That is enough to satisfy the Senate;
But for your private satisfaction,
Because I love you, I will let you know.
Calpurnia here, my wife, stays me at home. 　　　75
She dreamt to-night she saw my statue,
Which, like a fountain with an hundred spouts,
Did run pure blood; and many lusty Romans

49.　*consumed in:* consumed, swallowed by.

56.　*humour:* feeling (of fear); whim.

60.　*very happy time:* most opportune time.

70.　This line is delivered with the hint of a sneer. Decius must bring Caesar with him.

78.　*lusty:* lively, merry.

Came smiling and did bathe their hands in it.
And these does she apply for warnings and portents   80
And evils imminent, and on her knee
Hath begged that I will stay at home to-day.

Decius This dream is all amiss interpreted;
It was a vision fair and fortunate.
Your statue spouting blood in many pipes,   85
In which so many smiling Romans bathed,
Signifies that from you great Rome shall suck
Reviving blood, and that great men shall press
For tinctures, stains, relics, and cognizance.
This by Calpurnia's dream is signified.   90

Caesar And this way have you well expounded it.

Decius I have, when you have heard what I can say;
And know it now. The Senate have concluded
To give this day a crown to mighty Caesar.
If you shall send them word you will not come,   95
Their minds may change. Besides, it were a mock
Apt to be rendered, for some one to say
'Break up the Senate till another time,
When Caesar's wife shall meet with better dreams.'
If Caesar hide himself, shall they not whisper   100
'Lo. Caesar is afraid?'
Pardon me, Caesar; for my dear dear love
To your proceeding bids me tell you this,
And reason to my love is liable.

Caesar How foolish do your fears seem now,   105
    Calpurnia!
I am ashamed I did yield to them.
Give me my robe, for I will go.

[*Enter* BRUTUS, LIGARIUS, METELLUS, CASCA, TRE-
    BONIUS, CINNA, *and* PUBLIUS.]
And look where Publius is come to fetch me.

Publius Good morrow, Caesar.

Caesar   Welcome, Publius.
What, Brutus, are you stirred so early too?   110
Good morrow, Casca. Caius Ligarius,

80. *apply:* interpret.

89. *tinctures:* stains or colours used on coats-of-arms.

　　　relics: remembrances of a saint.

　　　cognizance: a mark of distinction.

96–7. *mock . . . rendered:* i.e., the kind of sarcastic remark one might expect.

103. *proceeding:* advancement or career.

104. *reason . . . liable:* i.e., my love for you is stronger than my reason (or sense of propriety) in daring to advise you in this way.

107. *robe:* the furred Elizabethan robe, or possibly some garment meant to resemble a toga.

Caesar was ne'er so much your enemy
As that same ague which hath made you lean.
What is't o'clock?

Brutus.   Caesar, 'tis strucken eight.

Caesar I thank you for your pains and courtesy.   115

[*Enter* ANTONY.]
See! Antony, that revels long a-nights,
Is notwithstanding up. Good morrow, Antony.

Antony So to most noble Caesar.

Caesar   Bid them prepare within.
I am to blame to be thus waited for.
Now, Cinna. Now, Metellus. What, Trebonius;   120
I have an hour's talk in store for you;
Remember that you call on me to-day;
Be near me, that I may remember you.

Trebonius Caesar, I will [*Aside.*] And so near will
    I be
That your best friends shall wish I had been further.   125

Caesar Good friends, go in and taste some wine
    with me
And we (like friends) will straightway go together.

Brutus [*Aside.*] That every like is not the same.
    O Caesar
The heart of Brutus erns to think upon.

[*Exeunt.*]

113. *ague:* fever.

118. *prepare:* i.e., the wine.

122. *remember that you:* remember to.

127. i.e., both friends and enemies may appear "like" friends.

129. *erns:* grieves.

COMMENTARY

Scene two shifts from the home of Brutus to Caesar's house in the early morning of the Ides of March. The storm of the previous scene continues to rage. Just as the private side of Brutus was exposed in the last scene, here Shakespeare shows us the private side of Caesar. By showing in consecutive scenes, both men in their homes, in conversations with their wives, Shakespeare highlights the parallel lives of the two men. Both men have had sleepless nights; both have wives concerned with their well being; and, as the play progresses, Brutus will become more and more like the man he seeks to destroy.

The foreshadowing of Caesar's imminent death begins early on in this scene as Caesar comments on the dreams that have tormented his wife, Calpurnia, all night. Immediately following his revelations that Calpurnia has cried out in her sleep, "They murder Caesar," Caesar instructs his servant to have the priests sacrifice an animal for the purpose of determining the future. Obviously, Caesar is concerned with the possible portents in Calpurnia's dream and this bears out Cassius' claim that he has become quite superstitious lately. Alone, the private Caesar is a fearful man concerned with what the signs point to as an ominous future.

Upon Calpurnia's entrance, Caesar replaces his public mask and begins by speaking of himself in the third person. Even with his wife and in the privacy of his own chambers, Caesar is unwilling to cast off his god-like demeanor. If there had been a humble Caesar before this time, he is gone now, and in his place is a man who is promoting his own glorification. Calpurnia relates what she has heard of the strange events of the previous night. She speaks of lions giving birth in the streets and graves that have opened and "yielded up their dead." She tells of blood dripping upon the capitol and comets blazing through the heavens and Caesar discounts every single omen. (The sighting of a comet had always held the connotation of the death of a monarch.) In July (the month of Caesar's birth) of 44 B.C., four months after Caesar's death, a comet, so bright that it could be seen during the day, was observed for seven days in the skies above Rome. Octavius Caesar used the phenomena to encourage the myth of Caesar's deification.

When the servant appears, he informs Caesar that the priests insist that Caesar stay home today because there was no heart found in the morning's sacrifice, and still Caesar refuses to be swayed. Caesar is purposely tempting the Fates by denying every sign they have sent to him to prevent his death. He seems to recognize the hand Fate plays in the lives of ordinary men but pompously ignores it in reference to himself: "these predictions / Are to the world in general as to Caesar." Calpurnia, frightened and frustrated by Caesar's refusal to acknowledge the signs sent by the gods, accuses him of allowing his wisdom to be destroyed by his conceit. The moment Caesar acquiesces to Calpurnia and agrees to stay home,

The Capitoline and the Forum.
Gianni Tortoli/Ancient Art & Architecture Collection Ltd.

Decius makes his entrance. His plan (to make sure that Caesar goes to the capitol) is in immediate danger of being thwarted. Decius wants to know why Caesar is not planning to go to the Capitol, and Caesar relates Calpurnia's dream to him. Decius, as promised, is a master of manipulation, and he begins to work his sorcery on Caesar by appealing to his vanity. He tells Caesar that "This dream is all amiss interpreted," and, with those few words, Decius articulates one of the major themes present in *Julius Caesar*, the manipulation of both fact and fallacy to achieve one's own end.

Julius Caesar and the Conspirators.
Mary Evans Picture Library

So much in this play is misinterpreted by so many, and the distortions are often a result of the characters' ego-driven desire to be proven right. The conspirators misconstrue the feelings of the common people towards Caesar. Casca, Cassius, and Caesar all confuse the signs and omens of the storm. Brutus continually misinterprets people and situations, and Cassius will die when he misinterprets a message at the end of the play. In this particular instance, Decius, appealing to Caesar's vanity, reinterprets Calpurnia's dream from something ominous into something fortuitous. Instead of interpreting Caesar's blood pouring from the statue as a sign of his impending death, Decius declares that the blood is a sign that Caesar provides the nourishment that will heal Rome and its people. In a clever display of flattery, Decius imposes religious connotations on the dream, suggesting that the people of Rome, rather than rejoicing in Caesar's spilt blood, are actually searching for "tinctures, stains, relics, and cognizance." The reference to religious icons places Caesar in the shadow of

sainthood, referring to the belief that handkerchiefs dipped in the blood of martyrs had healing properties. Just as Caesar's death is foreshadowed in Calpurnia's dream, Decius foreshadows Caesar's eventual martyrdom and rise to virtual sainthood in his ironic interpretation of the dream's symbolism.

Not wanting to risk the chance that Caesar may still refuse to go to the Capitol, Decius reminds him that the Senate is planning to give him a crown that day. He also warns Caesar that the Senators might possibly ridicule him if he stays home because his wife has had a bad dream. Caesar is swayed and, just as he agrees to leave for the Capitol, the other conspirators enter the scene.

Interestingly, Cassius is conspicuously missing from the list of conspirators named in the stage directions. Considering his insistence in the previous scene that "we will all of us be there to fetch him," it seems most strange that Cassius would not be among his co-conspirators at such a crucial moment. Perhaps Cassius is aware that Caesar does not trust him and so he makes the decision to stay away in order to not arouse Caesar's suspicion. After close examination of the play, textual scholars such as Fredson Bowers suggest that the parts of Cassius and Ligarius were played by the same actor. In scenes where Cassius appears, Ligarius is not on stage, and when Ligarius is seen, Cassius is missing. In this scene, Ligarius is listed as present in the stage directions and Publius, a character unknown up to this point has the honor of speaking first to Caesar.

Caesar affably welcomes the conspirators into his home and invites them to share wine with him. Again, the biblical reference to the Last Supper is obvious as Caesar shares wine with the men who will betray him. The scene also, once again, establishes parallels between Caesar and Brutus. In addition to the aspects already pointed out, both men are gracious hosts; they both are swayed easily by flattery and fatally trust the words and friendship of the conspirators.

Act II, Scene 3

Artimedorus has learned of the plot to murder Caesar. He writes a letter naming the conspirators, which he intends to give to Caesar as he passes on the way to the Capitol.

ACT II, SCENE 3.
A street.

[*Enter* ARTEMIDORUS, *reading a paper.*]

Artemidorus "Caesar, beware of Brutus; take heed
of Cassius; come not near Casca; have an eye to
Cinna; trust not Trebonius; mark well Metellus
Cimber; Decius Brutus loves thee not; thou hast
wronged Caius Ligarius. There is but one mind in   5
all these men, and it is bent against Caesar. If thou
beest not immortal, look about you. Security gives
way to conspiracy. The mighty gods defend thee!
                                         Thy lover,
                                         Artemidorus." 10

Here will I stand till Caesar pass along
And as a suitor will I give him this.
My heart laments that virtue cannot live
Out of the teeth of emulation.
If thou read this, O Caesar, thou mayest live;   15
If not, the Fates with traitors do contrive. [*Exit.*]

NOTES

7. *Security:* i.e., an unwarranted sense of security.

9. *lover:* friend.

12. *suitor:* petitioner.

14. *Out . . . emulation:* i.e., safe from the bite of envy.

16. *Fates:* in classical mythology, the three goddesses who directed human destinies.

    contrive: conspire.

COMMENTARY

According to Plutarch, Artemidorus, a professor of rhetoric, taught, and thereby associated with, many of Brutus' confidants and thus knew of the plot against Caesar. Artemidorus, listing the conspirators by name, has put his information into a letter that he intends to pass to Caesar as he approaches the Capitol. His attempt to save Caesar illustrates that Caesar has supporters as well as enemies, and, for the first time in the play, the conspirators are referred to as "traitorous."

This short scene, allowing for the passage of time between Caesar's leaving home and arrival at the capitol, also serves to create dramatic tension. Even though the reader knows that Caesar will die, the letter builds the suspense and gives hope that this Caesar might survive.

Act II, Scene 4

Brutus has shared his secrets with his wife, Portia, and she is frantic to hear news from the Capitol. She is afraid her nervousness will give the plot away, destroying her husband. The Soothsayer encounters Portia on his way to warn Caesar one final time.

ACT II, SCENE 4.
Before Brutus' house.

[*Enter* PORTIA *and* LUCIUS.]

Portia I prithee, boy, run to the Senate House.
Stay not to answer me, but get thee gone!
Why dost thou stay?

Lucius   To know my errand, madam.

Portia I would have had thee there and here again
Ere I can tell thee what thou shouldst do there.   5
[*Aside.*] O constancy, be strong upon my side,
Set a huge mountain 'tween my heart and tongue!
I have a man's mind, but a woman's might.
How hard it is for women to keep counsel!
Art thou here yet?   10

Lucius   Madam, what should I do?
Run to the Capitol and nothing else?

Portia Yes, bring me word, boy, if thy lord look
   well,
For he went sickly forth; and take good note
What Caesar doth, what suitors press to him.
Hark, boy! What noise is that?   15

Lucius I hear none, madam.

Portia   Prithee listen well.
I heard a bustling rumour like a fray,
And the wind brings it from the Capitol.

Lucius Sooth, madam, I hear nothing.

[*Enter the* Soothsayer.]

Portia Come hither, fellow. Which way hast thou   20
   been?

NOTES

1.   *prithee:* pray thee

6.   *constancy:* strength, self-control.

8.   *might:* strength, i.e., a woman's strength.

9.   *counsel:* secret information. Portia has been told of the plot. That there seems to be no time at which Brutus might have told her is irrelevant. This sort of double-time was a convention of the Elizabethan stage, and the difficulty is never noticed during a performance.

17. *bustling rumour:* confused noise.

19. *sooth:* in truth.

S.D. The reappearance at this point of the Soothsayer who had already warned Caesar of the ides of March (I.2.18) heightens the tension.

Soothsayer At mine own house, good lady.

Portia What is't o'clock?

Soothsayer   About the ninth hour, lady.

Portia Is Caesar yet gone to the Capitol?

Soothsayer Madam, not yet. I go take my stand,
  To see him pass on to the Capitol.

Portia Thou hast some suit to Caesar, hast thou   25
  not?

Soothsayer That I have, lady, if it will please
      Caesar
  To be so good to Caesar as to hear me:
  I shall beseech him to befriend himself.

Portia Why, know'st thou any harm's intended
  towards him?

Soothsayer. None that I know will be, much that I   30
      fear may chance.
  Good morrow to you. Here the street is narrow.
  The throng that follows Caesar at the heels,
  Of senators, of praetors, common suitors,
  Will crowd a feeble man almost to death.   35
  I'll get me to a place more void and there
  Speak to great Caesar as he comes along. [*Exit.*]

Portia I must go in. Ay me, how weak a thing
  The heart of woman is! O Brutus,
  The heavens speed thee in thine enterprise!   40
  Sure the boy heard me. — Brutus hath a suit
  That Caesar will not grant. — O, I grow faint. —
  Run, Lucius, and commend me to my lord;
  Say I am merry. Come to me again
  And bring me word what he doth say to thee.   45

[*Exeunt severally.*]

25.   *suit:* message

29.   *befriend:* guard

34.   *praetors:* high ranking officials.

36.   *void:* empty.

41.   *Sure . . . me:* Portia suddenly remembers Lucius, who is standing near.

43.   *commend me to:* give my wishes for success to.

S.D.   *severally:* by separate entrances at either side of the stage.

COMMENTARY

Shakespeare continues to build the suspense that will lead up to Caesar's assassination. Waiting is a suspenseful activity, and Act II has been a continuous round of waiting: waiting out the storm, waiting for the conspirators to arrive, waiting for the dawn, waiting to go to the Senate, and now, Portia waits to hear news from the capitol. In this scene, Portia's frantic behavior leads the audience to believe that Brutus has indeed kept his promise to reveal all of his secrets to his wife. Portia commands Lucius to run to the Senate House, but she forgets to tell him why he is to go. In his confusion, Lucius does not leave and Portia seems almost surprised to see him still standing there. She quickly makes up a story concerning her worry about Brutus' health.

Using *personification*, a figure of speech where something not human is given human qualities, Portia calls upon constancy to give her strength and "Set a huge mountain 'tween my heart and tongue!" Having once pleaded to be made privy to the conspiracy, Portia is now burdened by Brutus' secrets. Fearing that she will betray her husband, Portia laments that despite her masculine mind she has only a woman's strength.

Portia's hysteria makes her imagine that she hears noises coming from the capitol and she is surprised and concerned to see the Soothsayer making his way to the Senate House. Having been with Caesar when he was originally warned by the soothsayer to "Beware the Ides of March," Portia must be struck by the significance of the earlier warning. Her anxiety grows because of what she knows will happen in the Capitol in a very short time. She questions the soothsayer, asking him where he has been and what time it is. Portia then asks the question most pressing in her mind: "Is Caesar gone to the Capitol?" The soothsayer assures Portia that he is not there yet and verifies Portia's intimation that he has a suit for Caesar. The soothsayer repeats his apprehension that something will happen today to Caesar and expresses his desire to speak to Caesar about his fears as he passes through the streets.

Portia, feeling faint and overcome by the emotional turmoil of the day, blames her woman's heart for her weakness. She offers a prayer for the success of her husband's enterprise and exits the scene. This is the last time Portia is seen on the stage, but it becomes evident later in the play that, like Caesar, she becomes an innocent victim of her husband's actions.

Notes

Notes

CLIFFSCOMPLETE

JULIUS CAESAR
ACT III

Cinna *O Caesar.*

Caesar *Hence! Wilt thou lift up Olympus?*

Decius *Great Caesar.*

Caesar *Doth not Brutus bootless kneel?*

Casca *Speak hands for me.*

Caesar *Et tu, Brute? — Then fall Caesar.*

Cinna *Liberty! Freedom! Tyranny is dead!*
Run hence, proclaim, cry it about the streets!

Act III, Scene 1

On the way to the Capitol, Caesar encounters the soothsayer. Caesar again ignores his warnings and when Artemidorus tries to give his letter to Caesar, Caesar refuses to read it until later. Cassius is nervous that the plot has been discovered but all progresses as planned. Inside the Senate, Metellus Cimber approaches Caesar to ask for enfranchisement for his banished brother. All the other conspirators approach Caesar one by one supposedly on behalf of Cimber's brother. Brutus is the last to approach. Caesar refuses to change his mind, claiming he is as constant as the Northern star. As planned, Casca is the first to stab Caesar. The other conspirators follow suit but Caesar refuses to die until Brutus renders the final cut. Caesar falls dead at the base of Pompey's statue and the senators, thrown into a state of confusion, run panicked into the streets. Antony sends his servant to ask permission for him to return to the Senate to hear the reasons for Caesar's murder. When he arrives, Antony pretends to befriend the conspirators, shaking their bloody hands. He asks permission to speak at Caesar's funeral and Brutus, against Cassius' wishes, gives him his consent. The conspirators leave to explain to the people why they killed Caesar, leaving Antony alone with Caesar's mutilated body. Antony's deep grief becomes apparent as he vows to revenge Caesar's murder. A servant arrives, informing Antony that Caesar's nephew, Octavius, is on his way to Rome.

ACT III, SCENE 1.
Rome, before the Capitol.

[*Flourish. Enter* CAESAR, BRUTUS, CASSIUS, CASCA, DECIUS, METELLUS, TREBONIUS, CINNA, ANTONY, LEPIDUS, ARTEMIDORUS, POPILIUS, PUBLIUS, *and the* Soothsayer.]

Caesar The ides of March are come.

Soothsayer Ay, Caesar, but not gone.

Artemidorus Hail, Caesar! Read this schedule.

Decius Trebonius doth desire you to o'erread
(At your best leisure) this his humble suit.   5

Artemidorus O Caesar, read mine first, for mine's
a suit

NOTES

3.   *schedule:* scroll. We know the contents from II.3.

That touches Ceasar nearer. Read it, great Caesar!

Caesar What touches us ourself shall be last served.

Artemidorus Delay not, Caesar! Read it instantly!

Caesar What, is the fellow mad?

Publius   Sirrah, give place.   10

Cassius What, urge you your petitions in the street?
  Come to the Capitol.

[CAESAR *goes to the Capitol, the rest following.*]

Popilius I wish your enterprise to-day may thrive.

Cassius What enterprise, Popilius?

Popilius   Fare you well. [*Advances to* CAESAR.]

Brutus What said Popilius Lena?   15

Cassius He wished to-day our enterprise might
        thrive.
  I fear our purpose is discovered.

Brutus Look how he makes to Caesar. Mark him.

Cassius Casca, be sudden, for we fear prevention.
  Brutus, what shall be done? If this be known,   20
  Cassius or Caesar never shall turn back,
  For I will slay myself.

Brutus.   Cassius, be constant.
  Popilius Lena speaks not of our purposes;
  For look, he smiles, and Caesar doth not change.

Cassius Trebonius knows his time, for look you,   25
        Brutus,
  He draws Mark Antony out of the way

[*Exeunt* ANTONY *and* TREBONIUS.]

Decius Where is Metellus Cimber? Let him go
  And presently prefer his suit to Caesar.

Brutus He is addressed. Press near and second him.

Cinna Casca, you are the first that rears your hand.   30

Caesar Are we all ready? What is now amiss
  That Caesar and his Senate must redress?

10. *Sirrah:* contemptuous form of address, except when used to a child.

S.D. An example of the spatial flexibility of the Elizabethan stage. The audience is to imagine a change of scene at Cassius' "Come to the Capitol." The actors, or Caesar, may go to the recessed inner stage.

19. *sudden:* quick.

21. *turn back:* i.e., return from this alive.

28. *presently prefer:* bring at once.

29. *addressed:* prepared.

Metellus Most high, most mighty, and most puissant
    Caesar,
Metellus Cimber throws before thy seat
An humble heart. [*Kneels.*]

Caesar   I must prevent thee, Cimber.   35
These couchings, and these lowly courtesies
Might fire the blood of ordinary men
And turn preordinance and first decree
Into the lane of children. Be not fond
To think that Caesar bears such rebel blood   40
That will be thawed from the true quality
With that which melteth fools — I mean sweet words,
Low-crooked curtsies, and base spaniel fawning.
Thy brother by decree is banished.
If thou dost bend and pray and fawn for him,   45
I spurn thee like a cur out of my way.
Know, Caesar doth not wrong, nor without cause
Will he be satisfied.

Metellus Is there no voice more worthy than my
    own,
To sound more sweetly in great Caesar's ear   50
For the repealing of my banished brother?

Brutus I kiss thy hand, but not in flattery, Caesar,
Desiring thee that Publius Cimber may
Have an immediate freedom of repeal.

Caesar What, Brutus?   55

Cassius   Pardon, Caesar! Caesar, pardon!
As low as to thy foot doth Cassius fall
To beg enfranchisement for Publius Cimber.

Caesar I could be well moved, if I were as you;
If I could pray to move, prayers would move me:
But I am constant as the Northern Star,   60
Of whose true-fixed and resting quality
There is no fellow in the firmament.
The skies are painted with unnumber'd sparks,
They are all fire, and every one doth shine;
But there's but one in all doth hold his place.   65
So in the world: 'tis furnished well with men,
And men are flesh and blood, and apprehensive;

---

33.   *puissant:* powerful.

35.   *prevent:* forestall.

36.   *couchings . . . courtesies:* grovellings and humble bowing.

38.   *turn . . . decree:* i.e., change what has been ordained and decreed.

39.   *lane:* pathway. Some editors print "law."

      fond: so foolish as.

40.   *rebel:* unstable, unmanageable.

41–46.   Shakespeare frequently uses these images of melting, thawing, and the fawning of a dog to express contempt or flattery.

51.   *repealing:* i.e., repealing the edict that banished his brother, giving him permission to return to Rome.

54.   *freedom of repeal:* permission to be recalled.

57.   *enfranchisement:* restoration of rights as a citizen.

60.   *Northern Star:* regarded as a symbol of constancy.

62.   *no fellow in the firmament:* no equal in the heavens.

67.   *apprehensive:* capable of reasoning.

Yet in the number I do know but one
That unassailable holds on his rank,
Unshaked of motion; and that I am he,   70
Let me a little show it, even in this —
That I was constant Cimber should be banished
And constant do remain to keep him so.

Cinna O Caesar.

Caesar   Hence! Wilt thou lift up Olympus?

Decius Great Caesar.

Caesar   Doth not Brutus bootless kneel?   75

Casca Speak hands for me. [*They stab* CAESAR — CASCA
     first, BRUTUS *last.*]

Caesar Et tu, Brute? — Then fall Caesar. [*Dies.*]

Cinna Liberty! Freedom! Tyranny is dead!
   Run hence, proclaim, cry it about the streets!

Cassius Some to the common pulpits and cry out   80
   'Liberty, freedom, and enfranchisement!'

Brutus People and senators, be not affrighted.
   Fly not; stand still. Ambition's debt is paid.

Casca Go to the pulpit, Brutus.

Decius   And Cassius too.

Brutus Where's Publius?   85

Cinna Here, quite confounded with the mutiny.

Metellus Stand fast together, lest some friend of
     Caesar's
   Should chance —

Brutus Talk not of standing! Publius, good cheer.
   There is no harm intended to your person   90
   Nor to no Roman else. So tell them, Publius.

Cassius And leave us, Publius, lest that the people,
   Rushing on us, should do your age some mischief.

Brutus Do so; and let no man abide this deed
   But we the doers.   95

[*Enter* TREBONIUS.]

---

69.   *holds rank:* keeps his position.

74.   *Olympus:* a mountain in Greece, presumed, the home of the gods; Caesar's implication is that he is a god.

75.   *bootless:* vainly.

77.   *Et tu, Brute:* And you too, Brutus? The phrase is not in Plutarch, but was conventionally associated with Caesar's assassination.

80.   *common pulpits:* public platforms.

83.   *Ambition's debt:* i.e., what Caesar owed to Rome because of his ambition.

88.   *standing:* resistance.

94.   *abide:* be responsible for.

Cassius   Where is Antony?

Trebonius Fled to his house amazed.
  Men, wives, and children, stare, cry out, and run,
  As it were doomsday.

Brutus   Fates, we will know your pleasures.
  That we shall die, we know; 'tis but the time,
  And drawing days out, that men stand upon.   100

Casca Why, he that cuts off twenty years of life
  Cuts off so many years of fearing death.

Brutus Grant that, and then is death a benefit.
  So are we Caesar's friends, that have abridged
  His time of fearing death. Stoop, Romans, stoop,   105
  And let us bathe our hands in Caesar's blood
  Up to the elbows and besmear our swords.
  Then walk we forth, even to the market place,
  And waving our red weapons o'er our heads,
  Let's all cry 'Peace, freedom and liberty!'   110

Cassius Stoop then and wash. How many ages
      hence
  Shall this our lofty scene be acted over
  In states unborn and accents yet unknown!

Brutus How many times shall Caesar bleed in sport,
  That now on Pompey's basis lies along   115
  No worthier than the dust!

Cassius   So oft as that shall be,
  So often shall the knot of us be called
  The men that gave their country liberty.

Decius What, shall we forth?

Cassius   Ay, every man away.
  Brutus shall lead, and we will grace his heels   120
  With the most boldest and best hearts of Rome.

[*Enter a* Servant.]

Brutus Soft! who comes here? A friend of Antony's.

Servant Thus, Brutus, did my master bid me
  kneel;
  Thus did Mark Antony bid me fall down;

96.   *amazed:* in consternation.

100.   *drawing . . . upon:* length of life, that men consider important.

104.   *abridged:* i.e., since we have done Caesar a service in reducing the time during which he might fear death, we are his friends.

108.   *market place:* The Roman Forum.

113.   There is here a pleasant irony that Shakespeare could not foresee, since he could never have predicted the vast popularity and wide dissemination of his work in the 400 years following his death. What would he have made, for example, of this version of the assassination:

CAEZAR. ET TU, BRUTE? Basi, anguka Caezar!

[Anakafu. Waiumbe na raia wanafoka wamepigwa bumbazi.]

CINNA. Uhuru! Uhuru!

It is taken from a translation of the play into Swahili.

114.   *in sport:* i.e., in the theatre; for entertainment.

115.   *Pompey's basis:* the base of Pompey's statue.

117.   *knot:* group (of conspirators).

119.   *forth:* i.e., go forth into the city.

120.   *grace his heels:* follow him with grace, or honor.

122.   *Soft!:* wait.

And being prostrate, thus he bade me say;   125
Brutus is noble, wise, valiant, and honest;
Caesar was mighty, bold, royal, and loving.
Say I love Brutus and I honour him;
Say I feared Caesar, honoured him, and loved him.
If Brutus will vouchsafe that Antony   130
May safely come to him and be resolved
How Caesar hath deserved to lie in death,
Mark Antony shall not love Caesar dead
So well as Brutus living; but will follow
The fortunes and affairs of noble Brutus   135
Thorough the hazards of this untrod state
With all true faith. So, says my master Antony.

Brutus Thy master is a wise and valiant Roman.
I never thought him worse.
Tell him, so please him come unto this place,   140
He shall be satisfied and, by my honour,
Depart untouched.

Servant   I'll fetch him presently. [*Exit.*]

Brutus I know that we shall have him well to friend.

Cassius I wish we may. But yet I have a mind
That fears him much; and my misgiving still   145
Falls shrewdly to the purpose.

[*Enter* ANTONY.]

Brutus But here comes Antony. Welcome, Mark
Antony.

Antony O mighty Caesar! dost thou lie so low?
Are all the conquests, glories, triumphs, spoils,
Shrunk to this little measure? Fare thee well.   150
I know not gentlemen, what you intend,
Who else must be let blood, who else is rank.
If I myself, there is no hour so fit
As Caesar's death's hour; nor no instrument
Of half that worth as those your swords, made rich   155
With the most noble blood of all this world.
I do beesech ye, if you bear me hard,
Now, whilst your purpled hands do reek and smoke
Fulfil your pleasure. Live a thousand years,

130.   *vouchsafe:* promise.

131.   *resolved:* satisfied.

136.   *Thorough:* common Elizabethan form of through.

untrod state: unknown state of things.

143.   *well to friend:* as a firm friend.

146.   *Falls . . . purpose:* is close to the truth.

152.   *let blood:* purged, as in a therapeutic blood-letting.

rank: unwholesome/swollen with disease. A pun on too high a rank.

155.   *made rich:* spoken with as much irony as Antony can here allow himself, as is line 163.

158.   *reek and smoke:* i.e., are stained with blood.

I shall not find myself so apt to die;   160
No place will please me so, no mean of death,
As here by Caesar, and by you cut off,
The choice and master spirits of this age.

Brutus O Antony, beg not your death of us!
Though now we must appear bloody and cruel,   165
As by our hands and this our present act
You see we do, yet see you but our hands
And this the bleeding business they have done.
Our hearts you see not. They are pitiful;
And pity to the general wrong of Rome   170
(As fire drives out fire, so pity pity)
Hath done this deed on Caesar. For your part,
To you our swords have leaden points, Mark Antony.
Our arms in strength of malice, and our hearts
Of brothers' temper do receive you in   175
With all kind love, good thoughts, and reverence.

Cassius Your voice shall be as strong as any man's
In the disposing of new dignities.

Brutus Only be patient till we have appeased
The multitude, beside themselves with fear,   180
And then we will deliver you the cause
Why I, that did love Caesar when I struck him,
Have thus proceeded.

Antony   I doubt not of your wisdom.
Let each man render me his bloody hand.
First, Marcus Brutus, will I shake with you;   185
Next, Caius Cassius, do I take your hand;
Now, Decius Brutus, yours; now yours, Metellus;
Yours, Cinna; and, my valiant Casca, yours.
Though last, not least in love, yours, good Trebonius.
Gentlemen all — Alas, what shall I say?   190
My credit now stands on such slippery ground
That one of two bad ways you must conceit me,
Either a coward or a flatterer.
That I did love thee, Caesar, O, 'tis true!
If then thy spirit look upon us now,   195
Shall it not grieve thee dearer than thy death
To see thy Antony making his peace,

161. *mean:* method, means.

169. *pitiful:* full of pity.

171. The "fire" phrase is proverbial; Brutus means that pity for Rome drove pity for Caesar out of the conspirators' hearts.

173. *leaden:* blunt.

174–175. *our . . . in:* i.e., both our arms, although they appear hostile, and our hearts, full of brotherly feeling, receive you.

178. *dignities:* honors and offices of state.

181. *deliver:* explain at length.

191. *credit:* i.e., the trust others may have in me.

slippery ground: reference to the bloody ground.

192. *conceit:* think of, consider.

Shaking the bloody fingers of thy foes,
Most noble! in the presence of thy corse?
Had I as many eyes as thou hast wounds,   200
Weeping as fast as they stream forth thy blood,
It would become me better than to close
In terms of friendship with thine enemies.
Pardon me, Julius! Here wast thou bayed, brave
    hart;
Here didst thou fall; and here thy hunters stand,   205
Signed in thy spoil, and crimsoned in thy lethe.
O world, thou wast the forest to this hart;
And this indeed, O world, the heart of thee!
How like a deer, stroken by many princes,
Dost thou here lie!   210

Cassius Mark Antony —

Antony   Pardon me, Caius Cassius.
The enemies of Caesar shall say this:
Then, in a friend, it is cold modesty.

Cassius I blame you not for praising Caesar so;
But what compact mean you to have with us?   215
Will you be pricked in number of our friends,
Or shall we on, and not depend on you?

Antony Therefore I took your hands, but was indeed
Swayed from the point by looking down on Caesar.
Friends am I with you all, and love you all,   220
Upon this hope, that you shall give me reasons
Why and wherein Caesar was dangerous.

Brutus Or else were this a savage spectacle.
Our reasons are so full of good regard
There were you, Antony, the son of Caesar,   225
You should be satisfied.

Antony   That's all I seek;
And am moreover suitor that I may
Produce his body to the market place
And in the pulpit, as becomes a friend,
Speak in the order of his funeral.   230

Brutus You shall, Mark Antony.

Cassius   Brutus, a word with you.
[*Aside to Brutus.*] You know not what you do. Do

---

202. *become me better:* suit me better, i.e., as Caesar's friend.

     close: make an agreement with.

204. *bayed:* surrounded by hounds.

     hart: deer, with a pun on heart.

206. *Signed . . . spoil:* i.e., smeared with the blood of thy slaughter. Technically, "spoil" refers to those parts of the hunted animal which were distributed to the hounds.

     lethe: in classical mythology, Lethe was a river in Hades, the waters of which induced forgetfulness. Here, the association is with death generally.

209. *stroken:* struck.

212–213. *enemies . . . modesty:* i.e., even Caesar's enemies would say as much as this; therefore, it is moderate in a friend.

216. *pricked:* marked on a list.

224. *regard:* considerations.

227. *And . . . suitor:* i.e., and now I ask.

230. *order:* ceremony.

not consent
That Antony speak in his funeral.
Know you how much the people may be moved
By that which he will utter?   235

Brutus [*Aside to Cassius.*] By your pardon —
will myself into the pulpit first
And show the reasons for our Caesar's death.
What Antony shall speak, I will protest   238. *protest:* announce.
He speaks by leave and by permission;
And that we are contented Caesar shall   240
Have all true rites and lawful ceremonies.
It shall advantage more than do us wrong.   242. *advantage:* benefit.

Cassius [*Aside to Brutus.*] I know not what may
      fall. I like it not.

Brutus Mark Antony, here, take your Caesar's body
You shall not in your funeral speech blame us,   245
But speak all good you can devise of Caesar;
And say you do't by our permission.
Else shall you not have any hand at all
About his funeral. And you shall speak
In the same pulpit whereto I am going,   250
After my speech is ended.

Antony   Be it so.
I do desire no more.

Brutus Prepare the body then, and follow us.

[*Exeunt all except* ANTONY.]

Antony O, pardon me, thou bleeding piece of earth,
That I am meek and gentle with these butchers!   255
Thou art the ruins of the noblest man
That ever lived in the tide of times.   257. *tide of times:* stream of time, or history.
Woe to the hand that shed this costly blood!
Over thy wounds now do I prophesy
(Which, like dumb mouths, do ope their ruby lips   260
To beg the voice and utterance of my tongue),
A curse shall light upon the limbs of men;
Domestic fury and fierce civil strife   263. *Domestic:* internal.
Shall cumber all the parts of Italy;   264. *cumber:* burden.
Blood and destruction shall be so in use   265
And dreadful objects so familiar   265. *so in use:* so common.

That mothers shall but smile when they behold
Their infants quartered with the hands of war,
All pity choked with custom of fell deeds
And Caesar's spirit, ranging for revenge, 270
With Ate by his side come hot from hell,
Shall in these confines with a monarch's voice
Cry 'Havoc!' and let slip the dogs of war,
That this foul deed shall smell above the earth
With carrion men, groaning for burial. 275

[Enter OCTAVIUS' servant.]
You serve Octavius Caesar, do you not?

Servant I do, Mark Antony.

Antony Caesar did write for him to come to Rome.

Servant He did receive his letters and is coming,
And bid me say to you by word of mouth — 280
O Caesar!

Antony Thy heart is big. Get thee apart and weep.
Passion, I see, is catching; for mine eyes,
Seeing those beads of sorrow stand in thine,
Began to water. Is thy master coming? 285

Servant He lies to-night within seven leagues of
Rome.

Antony Post back with speed and tell him what
hath chanced.
Here is a mourning Rome, a dangerous Rome,
No Rome of safety for Octavius yet.
Hie hence and tell him so. Yet stay awhile. 290
Thou shalt not back till I have born this corse
Into the market place. There shall I try
In my oration how the people take
The cruel issue of these bloody men;
According to the which thou shalt discourse 295
To young Octavius of the state of things.
Lend me your hand [*Exeunt with* CAESAR'S *body.*]

268. *quartered:* cut in pieces.

269. *custom . . . deeds:* familiarity with cruel deeds.

270. *ranging:* hunting.

271. *Ate:* classical goddess of destruction.

272. *confines:* localities.

273. *Cry 'Havoc':* the signal, given by the commander of a victorious army, for the total destruction of the enemy.

let slip: unleash.

275. *carrion men:* decaying corpses.

282. *Thy heart is big:* swelling with grief.

283. *Passion:* here, grief.

286. *seven leagues:* approximately 21 miles.

287. *chanced:* happened.

292. *try:* test.

294. *cruel issue:* the result of the cruelty.

296. *young Octavius:* he was between 18 and 21 years old in 44 B.C.

COMMENTARY

The dramatic tension grows as Caesar's inevitable march toward death progresses. He enters the stage followed by the conspirators and is intercepted by both the Soothsayer and Artemidorus. In a display seemingly designed to impress his public, Caesar haughtily dismisses the Soothsayer and, with a show of false modesty, refuses to read Artemidorus' note until later: "What touches us ourself shall be last served." By refusing to acknowledge the omens present in the previous evening's storm, the missing heart in the auguers sacrifice, Calpurnia's dream, the soothsayer's warning, and Artemidorus' note, it becomes obvious that Caesar's arrogance has triumphed over his wisdom. Any sympathy that the reader might have felt for his plight is now almost non-existent.

Caesar's earlier perception that Cassius is a great observer who sees through the deeds of men is especially significant in this scene. With a heightened sense of apprehension brought about by the fear of being caught, Cassius notices Artemidorus trying to pass his scroll to Caesar and, along with Publius, urges him to move on to the Capitol. He is then approached by Popilius who expresses his wish that "your enterprise to-day may thrive." Cassius feigns ignorance and pretends not to know what Popilius is speaking about, but his fear grows as he watches Popilius move toward Caesar's side. With the very real possibility of disclosure, Cassius swears to Brutus that if their plot is discovered he will kill himself rather than be arrested for treason.

Suicide, to a predominately Christian, Elizabethan audience, would take on a much different connotation than it had in ancient Rome. To Shakespeare's audience, and indeed to many readers even today, suicide is considered a mortal sin; an act against God and nature. In Elizabethan England, it was also an act against the government. A suspected victim of suicide would not be allowed to receive the final sacraments or be buried in sacred ground. Often, victims of suicide were buried at the center of a crossroads, because their spirits, thought to be unable to go to heaven, would wander the world. Many Elizabethans believed that if the body of a suicide victim was buried at a crossroads, the ghost of the victim would not know which direction to follow. All money and property belonging to the suicide victims would be confiscated by the state, leaving the surviving family humiliated and destitute.

From the Roman perspective, however, suicide was considered an act of heroism if it was done in an effort to avoid living a life that conflicted with the moral and ethical values held in esteem by the person committing the act. For Cassius, living under the tyranny of Caesar was unthinkable. Thus, death would become his only alternative. For many members of Shakespeare's original audience, Cassius' desire to die rather than be arrested for treason was an emotion they could identify with. The severed heads of men and women accused of treason against the Crown, more often than not, adorned the spikes along the castle walls in London.

Shakespeare's plays were written specifically for performance, and his stage directions are often indicated within the text rather than added to the script. Lines 25–26 represent an example of what is known as an implied stage direction. Cassius points out to Brutus that Trebonius has set into motion the next stage of the plot against Caesar: "Trebonius knows his time, for look you, Brutus, / He draws Mark Antony out of the way." This would indicate to an actor that he must engage Mark Antony in some way that would "draw" him from the stage.

With Mark Antony out of the way, Decius comes forward to put the last moves of the conspiracy into place. Metellus Cimber is to approach Caesar first to ask for pardon for his banished brother. Each conspirator in turn will then join with Cimber until Caesar is surrounded and Casca is assigned the job of being the first to stab Caesar. Caesar takes his place and prepares to address the business of the day.

As planned, Metellus Cimber approaches Caesar and asks for the reinstatement of his brother as a Roman Citizen. Caesar's arrogance reaches astounding proportions as he refuses Cimber's plea based on his distaste for flattery and his power to remain constant. Ironically, Caesar's tendency to be swayed by flattery was just witnessed in the preceding scene and his constancy is ambiguous at best. For example, he has just spent much of the previous scene vacillating between staying home or going to the capitol and faltering from one interpretation of Calpurnia's dream to the other.

Shakespeare is a master at showing both sides of an issue or a character, and it is possible to interpret Caesar's recent actions in other ways. The qualities that comprise a great leader is a major theme in *Julius Caesar,* and an issue that is often and hotly debated. Even though Caesar's arrogance seems to be the motivating factor in much that he does, it is also possible to look at his choices in another manner. With regards to Artemidorus' letter for example, Caesar refuses to look at it until later, because the matter within the letter is personal to Caesar. Possibly, this choice illustrates Caesar's propensity to put the issues of the people above his own concerns. Constancy is also an important quality in an effective leader. It is unjust to have one set of rules for friends and another set for everyone else. In his "Northern Star" speech, Caesar is maintaining a firm position based on the laws of Rome and the judgment passed on Metellus Cimber's brother by the ruling factions in the government. Mercy and compassion must figure into the laws of the land but is it not the leader's responsibility to maintain those laws as set down without displaying favoritism?

Caesar's choices can be argued to be either arrogant or admirable but it is his growing sense of his own deification that destroys the man. By comparing himself to Olympus, a mountain in Greece presumed to be the home of the gods, Caesar is publicly declaring a god-like presence within himself. However, instead of showing god-like mercy and compassion by pardoning Cimber's brother, Caesar chooses to exhibit the very human quality of fundamental stubbornness. By the time

Casca raises his hand against Caesar, it is almost a relief to the reader to bring an end to Caesar's egotistical hubris.

Despite Brutus' earlier instructions that Caesar's death should be as clean as possible, each conspirator takes his turn at Caesar. Having endured twenty-two stab wounds, the still standing Caesar, his lacerations pouring forth blood, becomes the fulfillment of Calpurnia's dream. It is the twenty-third wound, however, inflicted by Brutus, the man he loved and perhaps fathered, that causes Caesar's life force to vanish, and he falls dead to the floor. The sympathy of the audience immediately swings back to Caesar as the pathos of his last words — "Et tu, Brute? — Then fall Caesar" — echoes through the stunned and silent Senate.

Cinna breaks the eerie silence with his cries of "Liberty! Freedom! Tyranny is dead!" Chaos ensues and all but one senator run into the streets proclaiming the news of Caesar's assassination. In a brilliant stroke that in the middle of this carnage adds a decidedly compassionate edge to both Brutus and Cassius, Shakespeare leaves one aging senator alone on the stage with the conspirators. Brutus assures the frightened old man that he will not be harmed and Cassius worries that Publius might be hurt in the madness and suggests that he leave right away.

According to Plutarch, each member of the conspiracy, in order to be equally involved in the murder, had agreed to stab Caesar at least once. With twenty-three stab wounds, Caesar's body resembled more the hacked carcass than the sacrificial "dish for the gods" that Brutus had aspired to. Bladders or sponges full of animal blood were concealed under costumes and when Caesar was stabbed, the actor playing Caesar would be saturated in the blood. This sight, along with the very real and pungent smell of animal blood that would

Julius Caesar is assassinated in the Senate by Brutus and his companions.
Mary Evans Picture Library

permeate the Elizabethan the-atre, certainly made the sem-blance of the conspirators as butchers a very powerful and vivid image.

Part of the ceremony of the Lupercalian Festival that opened this play was the ritualistic sac-rifice of a goat. The blood of the animal would then be smeared on the bodies of young men. By washing their hands in Caesar's blood, the conspirators not only fulfill the final prophecy of Calpurnia's dream but also reen-act a "religious ceremony" that will allow Brutus to continue to believe that this act was more than just a murder.

Blood as a pervading image in the play is no more evident than it is at this moment in the script. The vision of Caesar's bleeding body will silently but forcefully dominate the next 450 lines of this act. Caesar's blood not only

*The assassination of Julius Caesar.
Mary Evans Picture Library*

flows across the stage but also now covers the arms and hands as well as the weapons of the murderers. As with almost every image in the play, this one can be interpreted in numerous ways. If the murder of Caesar was a barbaric deed done to further the personal agen-das of greedy, jealous men, then the blood on the hands of the conspirators is a sign of guilt. If, however, the murder is a sacrificial purging of the sickness that runs through the body politic of Rome, then the blood becomes a symbol of catharsis and purification.

Throughout the play, Brutus' poor political judgment has laid the foundation for the failure of the conspiracy. In this scene, the reader is also made privy to Brutus' naivete. Not only does Brutus convince himself that Caesar's murder was a sacrifice, making heroes of the conspirators, but he justifies the act as beneficial, rationalizing it by believing that he has actually saved Caesar from the terrible fate of having to spend too many years fearing death.

In the highly charged elation of the moments following Cae-sar's death, Shakespeare uses a dramatic construct that has come to be known as *metadrama* or *metatheatre.* Throughout many of his plays, Shakespeare makes reference to his belief that "All the world's a stage, / And all the men and women merely players" and he frequently uses the convention of the play-within-the-play in such works as *A Midsummer's Night Dream* and *Hamlet.* Metadrama is much like a pic-ture of a mirror that must reflect itself into infinity. Which is the real image and which is just a mere reflection? The reader is jolted from the suspension of dis-belief into a very different dimen-sion of theatricality, one that highlights the capricious and illusory nature of the theatre. Brutus and Cassius, casting themselves as the leading play-ers in this "lofty scene," can believe themselves to be heroes and, in a very real sense, by hiding behind the metaphorical mask of actors, absolve themselves from their horrendous deed.

Cassius' question, "How many ages hence / Shall this our lofty scene be acted over / In states unborn and accents yet unknown!" is prophetic in many ways. Shakespeare's play has been performed consistently for the almost 400 years since his death and in languages unheard and in countries undiscovered at the time the play was written. To modern readers it takes on an even deeper meaning, because history has continued to repeat itself with the assassinations of great leaders such as Ghandi, John Kennedy, and Martin Luther King, Jr. As long as men have power, there will be other men who will kill to gain it.

As the conspirators are preparing to leave the Capi-tol to explain their deeds to the masses, a servant sent by Mark Antony detains them. Up to this point in the play, Antony has been a minor character, one who raised more contempt than concern. Only Cassius thought of him as a possible threat. The frivolous Mark Antony seen in the earlier scenes of the play now transforms himself into a shrewd, clever, and astute politician.

Antony is aware enough to know that if anyone other than Caesar is to die, it will be him. So Antony sends his servant to the conspirators with a well-prepared speech to make sure it is safe to approach. The message, as related by the servant, foreshadows Antony's ability to manipulate both people and situations with his words. The first line of the message appeals to Brutus' vanity, calling him, "noble, wise, valiant, and honest." Cassius voices his misgivings but Brutus overrules him and allows Antony to enter the Capitol for an explanation of Caesar's murder.

Antony is shocked and dismayed to see the ravaged body of Caesar, but he knows he must bide his time and make friends with the conspirators if he is to avenge Caesar's death. Antony continues the running metaphor of both disease and blood when he asks, "Who else must be let blood, who else is rank." If the body politic is swollen with disease, then the blood of Antony may be required to purge the state, restoring it to health. Brutus assures him that the conspirators have no desire to harm him in any way. Cassius, with his usual political acuity, cuts through Brutus' offer of love and reverence to offer Antony the more practical and desirable proposal: a share of the power and perks in the new government.

Antony does not answer Cassius' offers but proceeds, in a show of friendship and respect, to shake the bloody hand of each of the conspirators. With Caesar's blood on his own hands, Antony evokes Caesar's spirit for the first time. Caesar's spirit will

Caesar dead.
Mary Evans Picture Library

pervade the remainder of the play, and, though his body is dead, his influence lives on. Again, Cassius interrupts Antony and insists upon knowing whether Antony is to be counted as a friend of the conspiracy. Antony gives an evasive answer and quickly changes the subject, asking for permission to speak at a funeral for Caesar. Brutus agrees immediately, but Cassius, having noticed Antony's evasive answers when questioned about his loyalty to the conspiracy, takes Brutus aside and cautions him not to make the mistake of allowing Antony to speak at the funeral. Brutus refuses to listen to Cassius' fears and proceeds to turn Caesar's body over to Antony with a set of instructions for his funeral speech.

It was not uncommon for the body of a man who had transgressed against the state to be left unburied in the City Square. The family would be dishonored by having to watch the unconsecrated body of their loved one eaten by dogs and picked at by birds. The conspirators, seeing Caesar as an enemy of the state, would have been justified in leaving Caesar's body in the square, so their agreement to allow him a proper burial was a generous concession. Brutus instructs Antony to "prepare" or clean Caesar's body, and wrap it in a fresh shroud before following them to the pulpit where Brutus plans to speak.

Left alone, Antony finally reveals his true feelings toward the men he calls "butchers." Calling on the gods, Antony curses both the conspirators and Rome. Using images that are both bloody and brutal, Antony invokes the spirit of Caesar and vows to revenge Caesar's murder by unleashing the most devastating and destructive forces of hell. As though his prayers are immediately answered, a servant enters with the news that Octavius Caesar, Julius' grandnephew, his only living relative and heir, is within 21 miles of Rome. Julius may be dead but another Caesar moves in quickly to assume his role and take his place.

Act III, Scene 2

Brutus addresses the people of Rome telling them that the conspirators killed Caesar because he was ambitious. The people seem to be satisfied with that explanation and cry out for Brutus to be "Caesar." Antony arrives with Caesar's body to address the crowd and Brutus departs, leaving Antony alone to deliver his funeral speech. Antony turns the crowd against the conspirators. The violent mob disperses, creating havoc and running the conspirators out of Rome. Antony receives the news that Octavius has arrived in Rome.

ACT III, SCENE 2.
The Forum.

[*Enter* BRUTUS *and goes into the pulpit, and* CASSIUS *and the citizens.*]

Citizens We will be satisfied! Let us be satisfied!

Brutus Then follow me and give me audience, friends.
Cassius, go you into the other street
And part the numbers.
Those that will hear me speak, let 'em stay here;   5
Those that will follow Cassius, go with him;
And public reasons shall be rendered
Of Caesar's death.

1st Citizen   I will hear Brutus speak.

2nd Citizen I will hear Cassius, and compare their reasons
When severally we bear them rendered.   10

3rd Citizen The noble Brutus is ascended. Silence!

Brutus Be patient till the last.
Romans, countrymen, and lovers, bear me for my
cause, and be silent, that you may hear. Believe
me for mine honour, and have respect to mine hon-   15
our, that you may believe. Censure me in your
wisdom and awake your senses, that you may the
better judge. If there be any in this assembly, any
dear friend of Caesar's, to him I say that Brutus'
love to Caesar was no less than his. If then that   20
friend demand why Brutus rose against Caesar,

NOTES

1.   *will be satisfied:* have a full explanation.

4.   *part the numbers:* divide the people.

7.   *public reasons:* (1) reasons for the public to hear, or (2) reasons having to do with the public good.

10. *severally:* separately.

13. *lovers:* dear friends.

15. *have respect to:* remember.

16. *Censure:* judge.

this is my answer: Not that I loved Caesar less,
but that I loved Rome more. Had you rather Caesar
were living, and die all slaves, than that Caesar
were dead, to live all freemen? As Caesar loved   25
me, I weep for him; as he was fortunate, I rejoice
at it; as he was valiant, I honour him; but —
as he was ambitious, I slew him. There is tears for
his love; joy for his fortune; honour for his valour;
and death for his ambition. Who is here so base that   30
would be a bondman? If any, speak; for him I have
offended. Who is here so rude that would not be a
Roman? If any, speak; for him have I offended.
Who is here so vile that will not love his country? If
any, speak; for him I have offended. I pause for a   35
reply.

All None, Brutus, none!

Brutus Then none have I offended. I have done
no more to Caesar than you shall do to Brutus. The
question of his death is enrolled in the Capitol; his   40
glory not extenuated, wherein he was worthy; nor
his offenses enforced, for which he suffered death.

[*Enter* MARK ANTONY *and others, with* CAESAR'S *body*.]
Here comes his body, mourned by Mark Antony,
who, though he had no hand in his death, shall receive the benefit of his dying, a place in the com-   45
monwealth, as which of you shall not? With this I
depart, that, as I slew my best lover for the good
of Rome, I have the same dagger for myself when it
shall please my country to need my death.

All Live, Brutus! Live, live!   50

1st Citizen Bring him with triumph home unto his
  house.

2nd Citizen Give him a statue with his ancestors.

3rd Citizen Let him be Caesar.

4th Citizen   Caesar's better parts
Shall be crowned in Brutus.

1st Citizen We'll bring him to his house with shouts   55
  and clamours.

31. *bondman:* slave.

32. *rude:* uncivilized, barbaric.

40. *enrolled:* officially recorded.

41. *extenuated:* understated.

42. *enforced:* overstated.

45. *place:* i.e., as a free citizen.

47. *lover:* friend.

Brutus My countrymen —

2nd Citizen   Peace! Silence! Brutus speaks,

1st Citizen Peace, ho!

Brutus Good countrymen, let me depart alone,
    And for my sake, stay here with Antony.
    Do grace to Caesar's corse, and grace his speech   60
    Tending to Caesar's glories which Mark Antony,
    By our permission, is allowed to make.
    I do entreat you, not a man depart,
    Save I alone, till Antony have spoke. [*Exit.*]

1st Citizen Stay, ho! and let us hear Mark Antony.   65

3rd Citizen Let him go up into the public chair.
    We'll hear him, noble Antony, go up.

Antony For Brutus sake I am beholding to you.

[ANTONY *goes into the pulpit.*]

4th Citizen What does he say of Brutus?

3rd Citizen   He says for Brutus' sake
    He finds himself beholding to us all.   70

4th Citizen 'Twere best he speak no harm of
        Brutus here!

1st Citizen This Caesar was a tyrant.

3rd Citizen   Nay, that's certain.
    We are blest that Rome is rid of him.

2nd Citizen Peace! Let us hear what Antony can say.

Antony You gentle Romans —   75

All   Peace, ho! Let us hear him.

Antony Friends, Romans, countrymen, lend me
        your ears;
    I come to bury Caesar, not to praise him.
    The evil that men do lives after them;
    The good is oft interred with their bones.
    So let it be with Caesar. The noble Brutus   80
    Hath told you Caesar was ambitious.
    If it were so, it was a grievous fault,
    And grievously hath Caesar answered it.

60. *grace:* i.e., treat with respect both Caesar's body and the speech which Antony is about to make.

68. *beholding:* indebted.

83. *answered it:* paid the penalty for it.

Here under leave of Brutus and the rest
(For Brutus is an honourable man;   85
So are they all, all honourable men),
Come I to speak in Caesar's funeral.
He was my friend, faithful and just to me;
But Brutus says he was ambitious,
And Brutus is an honourable man.   90
He hath brought many captives home to Rome,
Whose ransoms did the general coffers fill.
Did this in Caesar seem ambitious?
When that the poor have cried, Caesar hath wept;
Ambition should be made of sterner stuff.   95
Yet Brutus says he was ambitious;
And Brutus is an honourable man.
You all did see that on the Lupercal
I thrice presented him a kingly crown,
Which he did thrice refuse. Was this ambition?   100
Yet Brutus says he was ambitious;
And sure he is an honourable man.
I speak not to disprove what Brutus spoke,
But here I am to speak what I do know.
You all did love him once, not without cause.   105
What cause withholds you then to mourn for him?
O judgment, thou art fled to brutish beasts,
And men have lost their reason! Bear with me.
My heart is in the coffin there with Caesar,
And I must pause till it come back to me.   110

1st Citizen Methinks there is much reason in his
    sayings.

2nd Citizen. If thou consider rightly of the matter,
  Caesar has had great wrong.

3rd Citizen   Has he, masters?
  I fear there will a worse come in his place.

4th Citizen Marked ye his words? He would not
    take the crown;   115
  Therefore 'tis certain he was not ambitious.

1st Citizen If it be found so, some will dear abide it.

2nd Citizen Poor soul! His eyes are red as fire
    with weeping.

92.   *general coffers:* public treasuries.

117.   *dear abide it:* pay heavily for it.

3rd Citizen There's not a nobler man in Rome than
    Antony.

4th Citizen Now mark him. He begins again to   120
    speak.

Antony But yesterday the word of Caesar might
  Have stood against the world. Now lies he there,
  And none so poor to do him reverence
  O masters! If I were disposed to stir
  Your hearts and minds to mutiny and rage,   125
  I should do Brutus wrong, and Cassius wrong,
  Who, you all know, are honourable men.
  I will not do them wrong. I rather choose
  To wrong the dead, to wrong myself and you,
  Than I will wrong such honourable men.   130
  But here's a parchment with the seal of Caesar.
  I found it in his closet; 'tis his will.
  Let but the commons hear this testament,
  Which (pardon me) I do not mean to read,
  And they would go and kiss dead Caesar's wounds   135
  And dip their napkins in his sacred blood;
  Yea, beg a hair of him for memory,
  And dying, mention it within their wills,
  Bequeathing it as a rich legacy
  Unto their issue.   140

4th Citizen We'll hear the will! Read it, Mark
    Antony.

All The will, the will! We will hear Caesar's will!

Antony Have patience, gentle friends; I must not
    read it.
  It is not meet you know how Caesar loved you.
  You are not wood, you are not stones, but men;   145
  And being men, hearing the will of Caesar,
  It will inflame you, it will make you mad.
  'Tis good you know not that you are his heirs;
  For if you should, O, what would come of it?

4th Citizen Read the will! We'll hear it, Antony!
  You shall read us the will, Caesar's will!   150

Antony Will you be patient? Will you stay awhile?
  I have o'ershot myself to tell you of it.

---

123. *none so poor:* none humble enough. Antony speaks with heavy irony here — meaning, apparently you are too great to show reverence for Caesar.

132. *closet:* private chamber.

133. *commons:* ordinary citizens.

      testament: will.

136. *napkins:* handkerchiefs.

144. *meet:* proper, right.

153. *o'ershot:* said too much.

I fear I wrong the honourable men
Whose daggers have stabbed Caesar; I do fear it.

4th Citizen They were traitors. Honourable men!   155

All The will! The testament!

2nd Citizen They were villains, murderers! The
will! Read the will!

Antony You will compel me then to read the will?
Then make a ring about the corse of Caesar   160
And let me show you him that made the will.
Shall I descend? and will you give me leave?

All Come down.

2nd Citizen Descend.

3rd Citizen You shall have leave.   165

[ANTONY *comes down.*]

4th Citizen A ring! Stand round.

1st Citizen Stand from the hearse! Stand from
the body!

2nd Citizen Room for Antony, most noble Antony!

Antony Nay, press not so upon me. Stand far off.

All Stand back! Room! Bear back!   170

Antony If you have tears, prepare to shed them now.
You all do know this mantle. I remember
The first time ever Caesar put it on.
'Twas on a summer's evening in his tent.
That day he overcame the Nervii.   175
Look, in this place ran Cassius' dagger through.
See what a rent the envious Casca made.
Through this the well beloved Brutus stabbed;
And as he plucked his cursed steel away,
Mark how the blood of Caesar followed it,   180
As rushing out of doors to be resolved
If Brutus so unkindly knocked or no;
For Brutus, as you know, was Caesar's angel.
Judge, O you gods, how dearly Caesar loved him!
This was the most unkindest cut of all;   185
For when the noble Caesar saw him stab,

167. *hearse:* bier; coffin.

172. *mantle:* toga; cloak.

177. *rent:* tear; hole.

181. *to be resolved:* to make certain.

183. *angel:* most favored companion.

185. *most unkindest:* most unnatural; an emphatic
double superlative.

Ingratitude, more strong than traitors' arms,
Quite vanquished him. Then burst his mighty heart;
And in his mantle muffling up his face,
Even at the base of Pompey's statue   190
(Which all the while ran blood) great Caesar fell.
O what a fall was there, my countrymen!
Then, and you, and all of us fell down,
Whilst bloody treason flourished over us.
O, now you weep, and I perceive you feel   195
The dint of pity. These are gracious drops.
Kind souls, what weep you when you but behold
Our Caesar's vesture wounded? Look you here!
Here is himself, marred as you see with traitors.

1st Citizen O piteous spectacle!   200

2nd Citizen O noble Caesar!

3rd Citizen O woeful day!

4th Citizen O traitors, villains!

1st Citizen O most bloody sight!

2nd Citizen We will be revenged.   205

All Revenge! About! Sneak! Burn! Fire!
  Kill! Slay!
 Let not a traitor live!

Antony Stay, countrymen.

1st Citizen Peace there! Hear the noble Antony.

2nd Citizen We'll hear him, we'll follow him, we'll 210
  die with him!

Antony Good friends, sweet friends, let me not
  stir you up
To such a sudden flood of mutiny.
They that have done this deed are honourable.
What private griefs they have, alas, I know not,
That made them do it. They are wise and honourable, 215
And will no doubt with reasons answer you.
I came not, friends, to steal away your hearts.
I am no orator, as Brutus is,
But (as you know me all) a plain blunt man
That love my friend; and that they know full well 220

196. *dint:* impression, as in dent.

   gracious: full of grace, honorable.

199. *marred:* mutilated.

214. *private griefs:* personal grievances. Antony suggests
that there may be some.

That gave me public leave to speak of him.
For I have neither writ, nor words, nor worth,
Action, nor utterance, nor the power of speech
To stir men's blood. I only speak right on.
I tell you that which you yourselves do know,   225
Show you sweet Caesar's wounds, poor poor dumb
   mouths,
And bid them speak for me. But were I Brutus,
And Brutus Antony, there were an Antony
Would ruffle up your spirits, and put a tongue
In every wound of Caesar that should move   230
The stones of Rome to rise and mutiny.

All We'll mutiny.

1st Citizen   We'll burn the house of Brutus.

3rd Citizen Away then! Come, seek the conspirators.

Antony Yet hear me, countrymen. Yet hear me
   speak.

All Peace, ho! Hear Antony, most noble Antony!   235

Antony Why friends, you go to do you know not
   what.
Wherein hath Caesar thus deserved your loves?
Alas, you know not! I must tell you then.
You have forgot the will I told you of.

All Most true! The will! Let's stay and hear the   240
   will.

Antony Here is the will, and under Caesar's seal.
To every Roman citizen he gives,
To every several man, seventy-five drachmas.

2nd Citizen Most noble Caesar! We'll revenge his
   death.

3rd Citizen O royal Caesar!   245

Antony Hear me with patience.

All Peace, ho!

Antony Moreover he hath left you all his walks,
His private arbors, and new-planted orchards,
On this side Tiber; he hath left them you,   250
And to your heirs for ever — common pleasures,

---

221. *public . . . speak:* leave to speak in public.

222. *writ:* a speech prepared, or written out. Many editors print "wit."

223. *Action:* use of gesture.

    utterance: verbal delivery.

229. *ruffle up:* raise in anger, as a dog's ruff.

243. *seventy-five drachmas:* Today, about $30.

248. *his walks:* see note at I.2.155.

251. *common pleasures:* public gardens.

To walk abroad and recreate yourselves.
Here was a Caesar! When comes such another?

1st Citizen Never, never! Come away, away!
We'll burn his body in the holy place   255
And with the brands fire the traitors' houses.
Take up the body.

2nd Citizen Go fetch fire!

3rd Citizen Pluck down benches!

4th Citizen Pluck down forms, windows, anything!   260

[*Exit citizens with the body.*]

Antony Now let it work. Mischief, thou art afoot,
Take thou what course thou wilt.
[*Enter servant.*]
                                    How now, fellow?

Servant Sir, Octavia is already come to Rome.

Antony Where is he?

Servant He and Lepidus are at Caesar's house.   265

Antony And thither will I straight to visit him.
He comes upon a wish. Fortune is merry,
And in this mood will give us anything.

Servant I heard him say Brutus and Cassius
Are rid like madmen through the gates of Rome.   270

Antony Belike they had some notice of the people,
How I had moved them. Bring me to Octavius. [*Exeunt.*]

255. *the holy place:* among the sacred temples of Rome.

260. *forms:* benches.

windows: shutters.

267. *upon a wish:* just as I wished it.

270. *Are rid:* have ridden.

271. *notice:* news. This comes from Antony as a grim understatement.

COMMENTARY

Historically, Julius Caesar's funeral took place on March 20, five days after his assassination. However, Shakespeare has taken dramatic license and compressed approximately six weeks of events into a single scene that takes place in the Forum. During the five days between Caesar's death and his funeral, the actual conspirators were quick to place themselves into positions of powers, assigning themselves heads of provinces such as Macedonia, Syria, and Asia Minor.

Shakespeare's version of the story has the conspirators going directly to the Forum to explain to the angry crowd why they felt it necessary to eliminate Caesar. This scene is one of the most brilliant examples in dramatic literature of the power of words to manipulate both intellect and emotion. As planned, Brutus is the first to speak.

Caesar's Forum.
Ronald Sheridan/Ancient Art & Architecture Collection Ltd.

Brutus' speech is written in simple, balanced prose, a much more logical and straightforward style than that of poetry. He begins by reminding the people that he is an honorable man and assumes the crowd will make the connection between an honorable man and an honorably motivated deed. Shakespeare creates rhythm in Brutus' speech through the use of *parallelism* (the repetition of words, phrases or sentences that have the same grammatical structure). This rhetorical tool is used to reinforce an idea or concept by making it memorable to an audience, but Brutus weakens his case by relying on merely technical tools to make his suit to the crowd. Brutus' speech is void of passion, appealing to the crowd's sense of reason and mistakenly deeming them his intellectual equals. His questions to the crowd are rhetorical in nature; thus, no answer is really expected. Politicians and other orators often use rhetorical questioning to manipulate an audience into believing they have made up their own minds about an issue when it has actually already been decided for them. Rather than aiming to reach the mob's emotions on a personal level, Brutus appeals to the abstract ideal of patriotism and offers to sacrifice himself for Rome. The bottom line, however, is that there is only one explanation offered to justify the need for Caesar's assassination: He was ambitious. Brutus makes no attempt to explain in what ways Caesar was ambitious but expects the crowd to take him at his word because he is an honorable man.

Again, Brutus demonstrates his almost absurd inability to read people and situations. He wants to believe that the common people of Rome are all noble, moral people with an unquestioning sense of patriotism but, as seen in the opening scene of the play, that is not the case. The commoners are often coarse, easily manipulated, and more interested in personal pleasures than public politics. It is obvious that the crowd does not grasp the reasoning behind the actions of the conspirators when they offer to crown Brutus, erect statues of him, and declare, "Let him be Caesar." Ironically, the crowd seeks to replace Caesar with the man who killed him; to create a new dictator from the one who attempted to eliminate the previous one. Brutus, however, chooses to ignore the callings and, feeling he has sufficiently convinced the crowd that the action of the conspirators was necessary, confidently but naively, leaves the pulpit to Antony. His trust in Antony is as misplaced as his trust in the mob before him.

The exact climax of *Julius Caesar* has been debated for years. Some feel that the actual murder of Caesar is the climax, whereas others contend that the turning point occurs when Antony turns the crowd against the conspirators. Obviously, the death of Caesar is a moment of emotional intensity that could qualify as the defining moment of the play, but the instant of greatest intensity and suspense occurs when Antony stirs the crowd to such frenzy that the downfall of the conspirators becomes inevitable.

Antony claims not to be a great orator, but his funeral speech is three times longer than the one given by Brutus and will, with its more emotionally effective use of poetry, move the people of Rome to violent acts of rage. As he begins to speak, Antony has the difficult task of commanding the attention of a crowd set against his purpose. He does this by first addressing them as friends and assuring them that his only intention is to

bury Caesar. It is obvious from the next line of the speech that Antony has listened carefully to Brutus' speech and found the explanation of Caesar's ambition to be a weak one. He picks up on the word, and repeating it consistently, begins to prove the contrary. He also, in keeping with the instructions Brutus has given him, reminds the crowd that Brutus is an honorable man. By alternating ironic references to Brutus' honor and nobility with real evidence of Caesar's lack of ambition, Antony forces the crowd to understand the subtext of his words without violating the conspirators' instructions not to speak ill of them. Without violating the rules established by Brutus, Antony destroys Brutus' only argument, that Caesar was ambitious.

Unlike Brutus' speech, which seemed almost sterile, planned, and memorized, Antony's speech suggests a more spontaneous approach, with attention being paid to the effect his words are having on his audience. When he suspects that he has completely undermined Brutus' singular argument that Caesar was ambitious, Antony begins to weep openly for his fallen friend. A man held in such high regard moves the crowd to silence and sympathy at this public display of emotion. Although Antony's tears may have been shed to purposely sway the crowd to his purposes, his grief over the loss of Caesar appears genuine and his feelings fuel the speech and thus, enflame the crowd.

After Caesar's assassination, Mark Antony rouses the mob with an impassioned eulogy.
Mary Evans Picture Library

Even though Antony has convinced the crowd that Caesar was not ambitious and the conspirators are not honorable men, he is not finished. If he is intent on letting "slip the dogs of war" he has more work to do. Historically, Antony, having convinced Calpurnia to give him free access to all of Caesar's papers, found Caesar's will the evening of the assassination. He intends to use it now in an effort to manipulate the crowd by appealing to its greedy nature. Having mentioned the will, the crowd is, of course, filled with curiosity and the more Antony declines to read the will the more insistent the crowd becomes.

Antony's next ploy to enrage the crowd draws on sentimentality and the use of visual aids. Closing in on Caesar's body, Antony shows Caesar's torn and bloody robe to the awed crowd. He tells them that Caesar wore that very cloak during the conquest of the Nervii and that he remembers the first time Caesar put on the robe. The Nervii was a very barbaric tribe living in Gaul but,

considering that Antony did not join Caesar in Gaul until three years after the defeat of the Nervii, it is highly unlikely that he actually remembered that particular battle, much less that particular robe. He then goes on to point out each tear in the mantle and identify the man who made each particular rent. Because Trebonius had taken Antony away from the Capitol before the assassination, making sure he was nowhere near, it is impossible for Antony to know such information. But he is not questioned, and the crowd is enraptured by his every word. Moving to the cut that he claims Brutus made, Antony describes it as "the most unkindest cut of all." If, as Plutarch suggests, Brutus stabbed Caesar in the genitals, this is perhaps the only accurate statement Antony has made in the past few lines.

Before Brutus left the Capitol, having turned the body of Caesar over to Antony, he had instructed Antony to "prepare the body." By that, Brutus meant for Antony to bathe Caesar's body, dress the wounds so they would not seep, and wrap the body in a fresh shroud. But Antony intentionally chose not to do this. He leaves Caesar's body in the same condition that he found it, and he now shows that pitiful sight to the crowd. In this highly charged moment, the people of Rome are moved to tears of rage and sorrow, but Antony is not yet quite satisfied with the crowd's emotional intensity. Now is the moment to remind the people of Caesar's will and its contents. Informing the crowd of Caesar's generosity is the explosive fuel that enflames the mob into the frenzy that Antony desires.

The image of fire as both a means of destruction and purification is powerfully intermingled in the violence and chaos unleashed in the final part of this scene. As Caesar's body is being sanctified through the ritual of cremation, the crowd takes firebrands from the funeral pyre to burn down the homes of the conspirators. Brutus and Cassius, along with the other conspirators, are forced to escape from Rome, the city they had desired to free.

Antony's actions of turning the mob into a violent, murderous force have often been criticized. But are his actions any worse than those of the treasonous and murdering conspirators?

Mark Antony's funeral speech over the body of Caesar.
Mary Evans Picture Library

Act III, Scene 3

Cinna the poet, encountering the hysterical mob, is mistaken for Cinna the conspirator and is murdered.

ACT III, SCENE 3
Rome, a street.

[*Enter* CINNA, *the Poet, and after him the citizens.*]

Cinna I dreamt to-night that I did feast with
    Caesar,
And things unluckily charge my fantasy.
I have no will to wander forth of doors,
Yet something leads me forth.

1st Citizen What is your name?   5

2nd Citizen Whither are you going?

3rd Citizen Where do you dwell?

4th Citizen Are you a married man or a bachelor?

2nd Citizen Answer every man directly.

1st Citizen Ay, and briefly.   10

4th Citizen Ay, and wisely.

3rd Citizen Ay, and truly, you were best.

Cinna What is my name? Whither am I going?
Where do I dwell? Am I a married man or a
bachelor? Then, to answer every man directly and   15
briefly, wisely and truly: wisely I say, I am a
bachelor.

2nd Citizen That's as much as to say they are
fools that marry. You'll bear me a bang for that,
I fear. Proceed directly.   20

Cinna Directly I am going to Caesar's funeral.

1st Citizen As a friend or an enemy?

Cinna As a friend.

NOTES

1.   *to-night:* last night.

2.   *things . . . fantasy:* i.e., what has happened to Caesar makes me imagine I may share his fate ("feast").

19.   *bear me a bang:* get a beating from me.

2nd Citizen That matter is answered directly.

4th Citizen For your dwelling — briefly.   25

Cinna Briefly, I dwell by the Capitol.

3rd Citizen Your name, sir, truly.

Cinna Truly, my name is Cinna.

1st Citizen Tear him to pieces! He's a conspirator.

Cinna I am Cinna the poet! I am Cinna the poet!   30

4th Citizen Tear him for his bad verses! Tear
him for his bad verses!

Cinna I am not Cinna the conspirator.

4th Citizen It is no matter; his name's Cinna!
Pluck but his name out of his heart, and turn him   35
going.

3rd Citizen Tear him, tear him! [*They kill him.*]
Come, brands ho! firebrands! To Brutus', to
Cassius'! Burn all! Some to Decius' house and some
to Casca's; some to Ligarius'! Away, go!   40

[*Exeunt citizens with the body of Cinna.*]

35. *turn him going:* send him on his way.

COMMENTARY

The crowd, enflamed by Antony's passionate speech, is out of control and looking for revenge. The mob mentality that overpowers and replaces individual logic takes hold of the Roman people and the poet, Helvius Cinna, no relation to Cinna the conspirator, is one of the doomed innocents to be victimized by the unthinking mass. In a scene taken from the works of Plutarch, the crowd confronts the poet and demands to know his name. When told his name is Cinna, the mob disregards his cries that he is not the conspirator of the same name, and proceeds to tear the unfortunate poet to bits.

In addition to showing the consequences of a violent and bloodthirsty mob, Shakespeare might have chosen this particular episode from Plutarch to illustrate other points as well. An issue that turns up in many of Shakespeare's plays is the importance of a name. In *Romeo and Juliet* for example, Juliet asks, "What's in a name? That which we call a rose / By any other word would smell as sweet." In Act I of *Julius Caesar*, Cassius questions why Caesar's name should be sounded with more power than Brutus'. In this scene, Cinna is killed because of his name. The label or image assigned to something has become more important than the person or object being named. The word "peace" can be shouted over the mangled body of a slain leader, Portia can maim her leg in an effort to live up to her father's name, and the crowds are content to let Brutus be "Caesar." The name, not the reality of what is beneath it, takes on almost mythical proportions.

In times of civil unrest, truth seems to lose its importance and reality becomes relative to the perceiver. As people who use words to uncover truth, poets have no place in this world of chaos. It is symbolic perhaps that Cinna the poet, the *seeker* of truth, is murdered rather than Cinna the politician, who uses words to *hide* the truth.

Notes

Notes

JULIUS CAESAR
ACT IV

Poet *For shame, you generals! What do you mean?*
Love and be friends, as two such men should be;
For I have seen more years, I'm sure, than ye.

Cassius *Ha ha! How vilely doth this cynic rhyme!*

Brutus *Get you hence, sirrah! Saucy fellow, hence!*

Cassius *Bear with him, Brutus. 'Tis his fashion.*

Brutus *I'll know his humour when he knows his time.*
What should the wars do with these jigging fools?

Act IV, Scene 1

Antony and Octavius have formed the second Triumvirate with Lepidus. The three men are discussing who among their enemies should be eliminated and how they can cheat the people of Rome from the inheritance left to them in Caesar's will. Antony informs Octavius that Brutus and Cassius are forming their armies and that it is time for them to prepare for war.

ACT IV, SCENE 1
Rome, a room in Antony's house.

[*Enter* ANTONY, OCTAVIUS, and LEPIDUS.]

Antony These many, then, shall die; their names
are pricked.

Octavius Your brother too must die. Consent you,
Lepidus?

Lepidus I do consent —

Octavius   Prick him down, Antony.

Lepidus Upon condition Publius shall not live,
Who is your sister's son, Mark Antony.   5

Antony He shall not live. Look, with a spot I
damn him.
But, Lepidus, go you to Caesar's house.
Fetch the will hither, and we shall determine
How to cut off some charge in legacies.

Lepidus What, shall I find you here?   10

Octavius Or here or at the Capitol. [*Exit* LEPIDUS.]

Antony This is a slight unmeritable man,
Meet to be sent on errands. Is it fit,
The threefold world divided, he should stand
One of the three to share it?   15

Octavius   So you thought him,
And took his voice who should be pricked to die
In our black sentence and proscription.

Antony Octavius, I have seen more days than you;
And though we lay these honours on this man

6.   *spot:* mark (made by Antony on the list).

9.   *cut . . . legacies:* i.e., cut down the payment promised to the people in Caesar's will.

12.   *slight unmeritable:* of no merit.

14.   *the threefold world divided:* the division of the Roman Empire into Europe, Africa, and Asia.

17.   *black sentence:* i.e., death sentence.

proscription: list of those proscribed, or condemned.

To ease ourselves of divers sland'rous loads,   20
He shall but bear them as the ass bears gold,
To groan and sweat under the business,
Either led or driven as we point the way;
And having brought our treasure where we will,
Then take we down his load, and turn him off   25
(Like to the empty ass) to shake his ears
And graze in commons.

Octavius   You may do your will;
But he's a tried and valiant soldier.

Antony So is my horse, Octavius, and for that
I do appoint him store of provender.   30
It is a creature that I teach to fight,
To wind, to stop, to run directly on,
His corporal motion governed by my spirit.
And, in some taste, is Lepidus but so.
He must be taught, and trained, and bid go forth: 35
A barren-spirited fellow; one that feeds
On objects, arts, and imitations
Which, out of use and staled by other men,
Begin his fashion. Do not talk of him
But as a property. And now, Octavius,   40
Listen great things. Brutus and Cassius
Are levying powers. We must straight make head.
Therefore let our alliance be combined,
Our best friends made, or means stretched;
And let us presently go sit in council   45
How covert matters may be best disclosed
And open perils surest answered.

Octavius Let us do so; for we are at the stake
And bayed about with many enemies;
And some that smile have in their hearts, I fear,   50
Millions of mischiefs. [*Exeunt.*]

20.	*To . . . loads:* to rid ourselves of the burden of slander, i.e., Lepidus is to take the blame for some of their actions.
26.	*empty:* unburdened.
27.	*in commons:* on the public pasture.
30.	*appoint:* provide.
	store: a supply.
	provender: food
32.	*wind:* turn.
33.	*corporal motion:* the movement of his body.
34.	*taste:* measure or degree.
36.	*barren-spirited:* dull, lacking spirit.
36–37.	*feeds . . . imitations:* i.e., enjoys curiosities (curious objects), artificialities, and fashions. Some editors read "abject orts" (abandoned scraps).
38.	*staled:* having been made stale.
39.	*Begin his fashion:* are newly fashionable to him.
40.	*property:* thing or possession.
42.	*make head:* raise an army.
43.	*combined:* strengthened.
44.	*stretched:* used as fully as possible.
46.	*covert . . . disclosed:* how secret matters may be discovered and dealt with.
48.	*at the stake:* the image is from the Elizabethan sport of bear-baiting. The bear was tied to a stake and "bayed" about with dogs.
51.	*mischiefs:* hostile thoughts/harms or evils. The word carried a stronger meaning for the Elizabethans than it does for us.

COMMENTARY

Although it seems that little time has passed between the end of Act III and the beginning of Act IV, the actual time between Caesar's funeral and the forming of the Second Triumvirate was over a year and a half. In that time, Antony failed to win over the Senate and was defeated by Decius Brutus' army in Gaul. While Antony was away from Rome, Octavius Caesar convinced the Senate to recognize him as Caesar's rightful heir and had Mark Antony declared a public enemy. In the meantime, while Antony and Octavius were at odds with each other, Brutus and Cassius gathered their forces and amassed their power over the eastern portion of the Roman republic.

Knowing that it was possible for Rome to fall into the hands of the conspirators if Antony and Octavius continued to oppose each other, Marcus Aemilius Lepidus, a Roman general, successfully attempted to reconcile the two men. In November of 43 B.C., the three men met in Bononia and reached an agreement to form the Second Triumvirate, a three-man government comprised of Antony, Octavius, and Lepidus.

Act IV opens on an horrific note as Antony, Octavius, and Lepidus casually assemble a list of men who are to die. The list includes not only enemies of the triumvirate but friends and family members as well. The three men bargain with each other, offering the death of a nephew for the death of a brother. This gruesome game clearly illustrates the viciousness and atrocities created by ill-managed insurrection.

Motivated by his obsession to revenge Caesar's death, Antony's savage and unscrupulous character is further revealed as the scene progresses. In his passionate funeral speech, Antony used Caesar's will to enflame the crowd to do his bidding. Now, he looks for ways to cheat those same people of their legacies. From his comments concerning Lepidus, it becomes clear that Antony uses and manipulates people as easily as he used and manipulated words in his funeral oration. Antony's regard for humanity, except in terms of property and serviceability, is nonexistent.

Mark Antony.
Ronald Sheridan/Ancient Art & Architecture Collection Ltd.

This scene becomes a fascinating parallel to Act II, Scene 1, in which the conspirators also have a conversation about who should live or die. In contrast to the quick and ruthless manner of the triumvirate in choosing those to eliminate, the ineffectual, almost illogical manner used by the conspirators in discussing Antony's fate begins to look nearly noble. Although possibly spurred by jealousy in Cassius or a misplaced sense of honor in Brutus, the bottom line for the conspirators' attack on Caesar was for the betterment of their beloved Rome. This scene provides a sharp contrast between the motivations of Brutus and Cassius and those of Antony and Octavius and clearly illustrates that compared to the new triumvirate, Caesar was a rather harmless tyrant.

Act IV, Scene 2

Brutus, camping with his army in Sardis, has sent for Cassius. Brutus' servant informs Brutus that Cassius has received him in a polite but distant manner. When Cassius arrives, it is obvious that the friendship between the two men is strained and they move into Brutus' tent to discuss matters further.

ACT IV, SCENE 2.
Before Brutus' tent near Sardis.

[*Drum. Enter* BRUTUS, LUCILIUS, LUCIUS, *and the army.*
TITINIUS *and* PINDARUS *meet them.*]

Brutus Stand ho!

Lucilius Give the word, ho! and stand!

Brutus What now, Lucilius? Is Cassius near?

Lucilius He is at hand, and Pindarus is come
To do you salutation from his master.   5

Brutus He greets me well. Your master, Pindarus,
In his own change, or by ill officers,
Hath given me some worthy cause to wish
Things done undone; but if he be at hand,
I shall be satisfied.   10

Pindarus   I do not doubt
But that my noble master will appear
Such as he is, full of regard and honour.

Brutus He is not doubted. A word, Lucilius,
How he received you. Let me be resolved.

Lucilius With courtesy and with respect enough,   15
But not with such familiar instances
Nor with such free and friendly conference
As he hath used of old.

Brutus   Thou hast described
A hot friend cooling. Ever note, Lucilius,
When love begins to sicken and decay   20
It useth an enforced ceremony.
There are no tricks in plain and simple faith;
But hollow men, like horses hot at hand,
Make gallant show and promise of their mettle;

[*Low march within.*]

NOTES

S.D.   *the army:* on the Elizabethan stage, the army would have consisted of a few actors with swords following the leaders.

4.   *Pindarus:* accented on the first syllable.

6.   *greets me well:* i.e., with a worthy representative. It has been pointed out that Brutus is always courteous to his subordinates.

7.   *In . . . officers:* i.e., either through a change in himself, or through the fault of his officers.

8.   *worthy:* justifiable.

10.   *satisfied:* have things explained to my satisfaction.

12.   *regard:* respect.

13.   *A word:* i.e., fell me.

14.   *resolved:* fully informed.

16.   *familiar instances:* signs of familiarity or friendship.

17.   *conference:* talk.

21.   *enforced ceremony:* forced politeness.

23.   *hollow . . . hand:* insincere men, like horses who are eager at first.

S.D.   The "march" was generally a drum offstage, and a "low march" a drum beaten softly to indicate that the approaching army was still at some distance.

But when they should endure the bloody spur,   25
They fall their crests, and like deceitful jades
Sink in the trial. Comes his army on?

Lucilius They mean this night in Sardis to be
     quartered.
The greater part, the horse in general,
Are come with Cassius.   30

Brutus   Hark! He is arrived.
March gently on to meet him.

[*Enter* CASSIUS *and his powers.*]

Cassius Stand ho!

Brutus Stand ho! and speak the word along.

1st Soldier Stand!

2nd Soldier Stand!   35

3rd Soldier Stand!

Cassius Most noble brother, you have done me
     wrong.

Brutus Judge me, you gods! wrong I mine
     enemies?
And if not so, how should I wrong a brother?

Cassius Brutus, this sober form of yours hides   40
     wrongs;
And when you do them —

Brutus   Cassius, be content.
Speak your griefs softly. I do know you well.
Before the eyes of both our armies here
(Which should perceive nothing but love from us)
Let us not wrangle. Bid them move away.   45
Then in my tent, Cassius, enlarge your griefs,
And I will give you audience.

Cassius   Pindarus,
Bid our commanders lead their charges off
A little from this ground.

Brutus Lucilius, do you the like; and let no man   50
Come to our tent till we have done our conference.
Let Lucius and Titinius guard our door. [*Exeunt.*]

---

26.   *fall their crests:* lower their manes.
     jades: worthless horses.

27.   *Sink . . . trial:* fail in the test.

29.   *horse in general:* the cavalry.

31.   *gently:* slowly.

40.   *sober form:* restrained manner.

41.   *content:* calm.

42.   *griefs:* grievances.

46.   *enlarge:* give free expression to.

48.   *charges:* troops.

COMMENTARY

For the first time in the play, the location shifts from Rome to Sardis, the capital of Lydia, a kingdom in Asia Minor. Again, Shakespeare seems to draw a comparison between the forces of Antony and Octavius and Brutus and Cassius. Although there is evidence of power struggles beginning between Antony and Octavius in the previous scene, the two men remain united in their purposes. This scene clearly establishes the fact that the relationship between Brutus and Cassius has seriously deteriorated, reflecting a larger picture of discord within the republican cause.

The issue of friendship that pervades Julius Caesar is especially evident in this scene and the next. The word "love" and its variants occurs fifty-six times in the course of the play and here Brutus discloses that his friendship with Cassius is "cooling" and the love that had once been between them has begun to "sicken and decay." The breech between the two men is a direct result of the conflict between the realist and the idealist. Even in the horrific aftermath of the assassination, Brutus has not lost his naivete, and his personal principles still take precedence over his personal relationships.

Brutus' preoccupation with how situations appear to others is obviously still of great concern to him. When Cassius publicly accuses Brutus of wrongdoing, Brutus cuts him off and admonishes him for speaking so candidly before the armies. That the morale of the troops could be adversely affected by witnessing an argument between the two leaders is obvious, but it is also likely that Brutus would not want to be seen as out of control or have his faults recounted in a public setting. The fiery and passionate Cassius continues to subordinate himself to Brutus. At Brutus' request, Cassius subdues himself and the two men move within Brutus' tent to continue airing their frustrations.

In the 1623 Folio, there is no division between Scenes 2 and 3 in Act IV. The separation of the two scenes was actually executed by Alexander Pope in his edition of the plays published in the early 1700s. Pope's rationale for dividing the two scenes was that Brutus and Cassius move from one place to another. Because there were no major scenery changes possible on the stage of the Globe Theatre and there has been no evidence of tents set up on the stage as in *Richard III*, it is most likely that the other characters listed in the stage directions merely left the stage, leaving Brutus and Cassius alone to continue the scene. However, the majority of modern editors have retained the division of the two scenes.

Act IV, Scene 3

Brutus accuses Cassius of accepting bribes and the quarrel between the two men escalates until both men realize the futility of their anger. Brutus tells Cassius that Portia has committed suicide and the men make plans for the forthcoming war with Antony and Octavius. After the men leave Brutus' tent, Brutus is visited by the ghost of Caesar who tells Brutus he will see him at Philippi.

ACT IV, SCENE 3.
Within Brutus' tent.

[*Enter* BRUTUS *and* CASSIUS.]

Cassius That you have wronged me doth appear in
    this:
You have condemned and noted Lucius Pella
For taking bribes here of the Sardians;
Wherein my letters, praying on his side,
Because I knew the man, was slighted off.   5

Brutus You wronged yourself to write in such a case.

Cassius In such a time as this it is not meet
That every nice offence should bear his comment.

Brutus Let me tell you, Cassius, you yourself
Are much condemned to have an itching palm,   10
To sell and mart your offices for gold
To undeservers.

Cassius   I an itching palm?
You know that you are Brutus that speaks this,
Or by the gods, this speech were else your last!

Brutus The name of Cassius honours this cor-   15
    ruption,
And chastisement doth therefore hide his head.

Cassius. Chastisement?

Brutus. Remember March; the ides of March
    remember.
Did not great Julius bleed for justice sake?
What villain touched his body that did stab   20
And not for justice? What, shall one of us,
That struck the foremost man of all this world
But for supporting robbers — shall we now
Contaminate our fingers with base bribes,

NOTES

2.   *noted:* publicly disgraced.

4.   *letters:* in Shakespeare's writing, the word is often singular in meaning.

5.   *slighted off:* contemptuously dismissed.

8.   *nice . . . comment:* trivial error should be criticized.

10.   *itching palm:* avid desire for money

11.   *mart your offices:* i.e., make bargains or profits because of your powers.

16.   *chastisement doth therefore hide his head:* legal authority afraid to act because of Cassius' influence.

23.   *supporting robbers:* i.e., for supporting those who would rob Romans of their liberties.

And sell the mighty space of our large honours   25
For so much trash as may be grasped thus?
I had rather be a dog and bay the moon
Than such a Roman.

Cassius   Brutus, bait not me!
I'll not endure it. You forget yourself
To hedge me in. I am a soldier, I,   30
Older in practice, abler than yourself
To make conditions.

Brutus   Go to! You are not, Cassius.

Cassius I am.

Brutus I say you are not.

Cassius Urge me no more! I shall forget myself.   35
Have mind upon your health. Tempt me no further.

Brutus Away, slight man!

Cassius Is't possible?

Brutus   Hear me, for I will speak.
Must I give way and room to your rash choler?
Shall I be frighted when a madman stares?   40

Cassius O ye gods, ye gods! Must I endure all this?

Brutus All this! Aye, more. Fret till your proud
      heart break.
Go show your slaves how choleric you are
And make your bondmen tremble. Must I budge?
Must I observe you? Must I stand and crouch   45
Under your testy humour? By the gods,
You shall digest the venom of your spleen,
Though it do split you; for from this day forth
I'll use you for my mirth, yea, for my laughter,
When you are waspish.   50

Cassius   Is it come to this?

Brutus You say you are a better soldier.
Let it appear so; make your vaunting true,
And it shall please me well. For mine own part,
I shall be glad to learn of noble men.

Cassius You wrong me every way! You wrong me,   55
     Brutus!

25.	*the . . . honours:* i.e., the great scope we have in conferring honors.
26.	*grasped thus:* implied stage direction. The grasp shows act of greed.
27.	*dog and bay at the moon:* proverbial for something wasted or useless.
28.	*bait:* tempt to violence.
30.	*hedge me in:* restrict me.
31.	*practice:* experience.
32.	*make conditions:* to decide matters.
37.	*slight:* worthless.
39.	*way . . . choler:* scope to your anger.
40.	*stares:* glares or glowers with anger.
45.	*crouch:* bow.
46.	*testy humour:* irritable temper.
47.	*digest . . . spleen:* swallow the poison of your anger. The spleen was thought to be the source of anger.
52.	*vaunting:* boasting.
54.	*learn of:* both (1) discover the existence of, and (2) learn a lesson from.

I said an elder soldier, not a better.
Did I say 'better'?

Brutus   If you did, I care not.

Cassius When Caesar lived he durst not thus have
    moved me.

Brutus Peace, peace! You durst not so have
    tempted him.   60

Cassius I durst not?

Brutus No.

Cassius What, durst not tempt him?

Brutus   For your life, you durst not.

Cassius Do not presume too much upon my love.
    I may do that I shall be sorry for.   65

Brutus You have done that you should be sorry
      for.
  There is no terror, Cassius, in your threats;
  For I am armed so strong in honesty
  That they pass by me as the idle wind,
  Which I respect not. I did send to you
  For certain sums of gold, which you denied me;   70
  For I can raise no money by vile means.
  By heaven, I had rather coin my heart
  And drop my blood for drachmas than to wring
  From the hard hands of peasant their vile trash
  By any indirection. I did send   75
  To you for gold to pay my legions,
  Which you denied me. Was that done like Cassius?
  Should I have answered Caius Cassius so?
  When Marcus Brutus grows so covetous
  To lock such rascal counters from his friends,   80
  Be ready, gods, with all your thunderbolts,
  Dash him to pieces!

Cassius   I denied you not.

Brutus You did.

Cassius I did not. He was but a fool that brought
  My answer back. Brutus hath rived my heart.   85
  A friend should bear his friend's infirmities,

58.   *moved:* angered.

75.   *indirection:* dishonest dealing.

80.   *rascal counters:* cheap coins.

85.   *rived:* split in two.

But Brutus makes mine greater than they are.

Brutus I do not, till you practise them on me.

Cassius You love me not.

Brutus   I do not like your faults.

Cassius A friendly eye could never see such faults.   90

Brutus A flatterer's would not, though they do
     appear
As high as huge Olympus.

Cassius Come, Antony, and young Octavius, come!
Revenge yourselves alone on Cassius.
For Cassius is aweary of the world: 95
Hated by one he loves; braved by his brother;
Checked like a bondman; all his faults observed,
Set in a notebook, learned and conned by rote
To cast into my teeth. O, could weep
My spirit from mine eyes! There is my dagger,   100
And here my naked breast; within, a heart
Dearer than Pluto's mine, richer than gold.
If that thou be'st a Roman, take it forth.
I, that denied thee gold, will give my heart.
Strike as thou didst at Caesar; for I know,   105
When thou didst hate him worst, thou lovedst him
     better
Than ever thou lovedst Cassius.

Brutus   Sheathe your dagger.
Be angry when you will; it shall have scope.
Do what you will; dishonour shall be humour
O Cassius, you are yoked with a lamb   110
That carries anger as the flint bears fire;
Who, much enforced, shows a hasty spark,
And straight is cold again.

Cassius   Hath Cassius lived
To be but mirth and laughter to his Brutus
When grief and blood ill-tempered vexeth him?   115

Brutus When I spoke that, I was ill-tempered too.

Cassius Do you confess so much? Give me your
     hand.

Brutus And my heart too.

96.   *braved:* defied.

97.   *checked like a bondman:* scolded like a slave.

98.   *conned by rote:* learned by heart.

102.   Cassius (and Shakespeare) may have here confused Pluto, the god of the underworld, and Plutus, the god of wealth.

108.   *scope:* freedom.

109.   *dishonour . . . humour:* i.e., I shall take any insult as an effect of your mood.

112.   *much enforced:* violently or repeatedly struck.

115.   *blood ill-tempered:* unbalanced emotion.

Cassius   O Brutus!

Brutus   What's the matter?

Cassius Have you not love enough to bear with me
When that rash humour which my mother gave me   120
Makes me forgetful?

Brutus   Yes, Cassius; and from henceforth,
When you are over-earnest with your Brutus,
He'll think your mother chides, and leave you so.

[*Enter a poet, followed by* LUCILIUS, TITINIUS, *and*
LUCIUS.]

Poet Let me go in to see the generals!
There is some grudge between 'em. 'Tis not meet   125
They be alone.

Lucilius You shall not come to them.

Poet Nothing but death shall stay me.

Cassius How now? What's the matter?

Poet For shame, you generals! What do you mean?   130
Love and be friends, as two such men should be;
For I have seen more years, I'm sure, than ye.

Cassius Ha ha! How vilely doth this cynic rhyme!

Brutus Get you hence, sirrah! Saucy fellow,
hence!

Cassius Bear with him, Brutus. 'Tis his fashion.   135

Brutus I'll know his humour when he knows his
time.
What should the wars do with these jigging fools?
Companion, hence!

Cassius   Away, away, be gone!

[*Exit poet.*]

Brutus Lucilius and Titinius, bid the commanders
Prepare to lodge their companies to-night.   140

Cassius And come yourselves, and bring Messala
with you
Immediately to us. [*Exeunt* LUCIUS *and* TITINIUS.]

Brutus   Lucius, a bowl of wine.

---

120. *rash . . . me:* i.e., the quick temper I inherited from my mother.

133. *cynic:* ill-mannered fellow, with special reference to the philosophical school of Cynics who were generally critical of anyone else's behavior.

134. *Saucy:* insolent.

136. *I'll . . . time:* i.e., I'll attend to him when he chooses the proper time to speak to me.

137. *jigging:* here rhyming, contemptuously or empty and vulgar.

138. *Companion:* a contemptuous form of address.

[*Exit* LUCIUS.]

Cassius I did not think you could have been so
  angry.

Brutus O Cassius, I am sick of many griefs.

Cassius Of your philosophy you make no use   145
  If you give place to accidental evils.

Brutus No man bears sorrow better. Portia is dead.

Cassius Ha! Portia?

Brutus She is dead.

Cassius How scaped I killing when I crossed   150
  you so?
  O insupportable and touching loss!
  Upon what sickness?

Brutus   Impatient of my absence,
  And grief that young Octavius with Mark Antony
  Have made themselves so strong; for with her
    death
  That tidings came. With this she fell distract,   155
  And (her attendants absent) swallowed fire.

Cassius And died so?

Brutus   Even so.

Cassius   O ye immortal gods!

[*Enter* LUCIUS *with wine and tapers.*]

Brutus Speak no more of her. Give me a bowl of
  wine. [*Drinks.*]
  In this I bury all unkindness, Cassius.

Cassius My heart is thirsty for that noble pledge.   160
  Fill, Lucius, till the wine o'erswell the cup.
  I cannot drink too much of Brutus' love.

[*Drinks. Exit* LUCIUS.]

[*Enter* TITINIUS *and* MESSALA.]

Brutus Come in, Titinius! Welcome, good Messala.
  Now sit we close about this taper here
  And call in question our necessities.   165

Cassius Portia, art thou gone?

146.   *accidental evils:* evils that come by chance.

150.   *crossed:* opposed.

151.   *touching:* grievous. The word was stronger for the Elizabethans than it is for us.

152.   *Upon:* as a result of.

154–155. *for . . . came:* i.e., the news of their strength and her death came together.

155.   *distract:* out of her mind.

156.   *swallowed fire:* the detail is from Plutarch, who says she cast hot burning coals into her mouth and she choked herself.

159.   *unkindness:* enmity.

165.   *call . . . necessities:* examine our needs.

Brutus   No more, I pray you.
Messala, I have here received letters
That young Octavius and Mark Antony
Come down upon us with a mighty power,
Bending their expedition toward Philippi.   170

Messala Myself have letters of the selfsame tenure.

Brutus With what addition?

Messala That by proscription and bills of outlawry
Octavius, Antony, and Lepidus
Have put to death an hundred senators.   175

Brutus Therein our letters do not well agree.
Mine speak of seventy senators that died
By their proscriptions, Cicero being one.

Cassius Cicero one?

Messala   Cicero is dead,
And by that order of proscription.   180
Had you your letters from your wife, my lord?

Brutus No, Messala.

Messala Nor nothing in your letters writ of her?

Brutus Nothing, Messala.

Messala   That methinks is strange.

Brutus Why ask you? Hear you aught of her in   185
    yours?

Messala No, my lord.

Brutus Now as you are a Roman, tell me true.

Messala Then like a Roman bear the truth I tell;
For certain she is dead, and by strange manner.

Brutus Why, farewell, Portia. We must die,   190
    Messala.
With meditating that she must die once,
I have the patience to endure it now.

Messala Even so great men great losses should
    endure.

Cassius I have as much of this in art as you,
But yet my nature could not bear it so.   195

171.   *tenture:* meaning, information.

172.   *addition?:* i.e., with anything else?

173.   *proscription:* sentence of death.

       bills of outlawry: i.e., lists of those outlawed.

191.   *once:* at some time.

194.   *in art:* in knowledge (of the Stoic philosophy).

195.   *my nature:* i.e., my natural emotions or instincts.

Brutus Well, to our work alive. What do you think
  Of marching to Philippi presently?

Cassius I do not think it good.

Brutus   Your reason?

Cassius   This it is:
  'Tis better that the enemy seek us.
  So shall he waste his means, weary his soldiers,   200
  Doing himself offence, whilst we, lying still,
  Are full of rest, defence, and nimbleness.

Brutus Good reasons must of force give place to
      better.
  The people 'twixt Philippi and this ground
  Do stand but in a forced affection;   205
  For they have grudged us contribution.
  The enemy, marching along by them,
  By them shall make a fuller number up,
  Come on refreshed, new added, and encouraged;
  From which advantage shall we cut him off   210
  If at Philippi we do face him there,
  These people at our back.

Cassius   Hear me, good brother.

Brutus Under your pardon. You must note beside
  That we have tried the utmost of our friends,
  Our legions are brimful, our cause is ripe.   215
  The enemy increaseth every day;
  We, at the height, are ready to decline.
  There is a tide in the affairs of men
  Which, taken at the flood, leads on to fortune;
  Omitted, all the voyage of their life   220
  Is bound in shallows and in miseries.
  On such a full sea are we now afloat,
  And we must take the current when it serves
  Or lose our ventures.

Cassius   Then, with your will, go on.
  We'll along ourselves, and meet them at Philippi.   225

Brutus The deep of night is crept upon our talk
  And nature must obey necessity,
  Which we will niggard with a little rest.
  There is no more to say?

196. *alive:* which concerns the living.

197. *presently:* at once.

201. *offence:* damage.

205. *a forced affection:* loyalty compelled by force.

208. *By them:* by enlisting them.

209. *new added:* with new additions.

214. *tried . . . of:* tested thoroughly.

220. *Omitted:* missed, not taken.

224. *ventures:* investments in a voyage; the sailing metaphor is continued.

228. *niggard:* be stingy with or satisfy reluctantly.

Cassius   No more. Good night.
Early to-morrow will we rise and hence.   230

Brutus Lucius! [*Enter* LUCIUS.] My gown. [*Exit* LUCIUS.]
   Farewell good Messala.
Good night, Titinius. Noble, noble Cassius,
Good night and good repose.

Cassius   O my dear brother,
This was an ill beginning of the night!   235
Never come such division 'tween our souls!
Let it not, Brutus.

[*Enter* LUCIUS *with the gown.*]

Brutus   Everything is well.

Cassius Good night, my lord.

Brutus   Good night, good brother.

Titinius, Messala   Good night, Lord Brutus.

Brutus   Farewell every one.

[*Exeunt* CASSIUS, TITINIUS, *and* MESSALA.]
   Give me my gown. Where is thy instrument?

Lucius Here in the tent.   240

Brutus   What, thou speak'st drowsily?
Poor knave, I blame thee not; thou art o'erwatched.
Call Claudius and some other of my men;
I'll have them sleep on cushions in my tent.

Lucius Varro and Claudius!

[*Enter* VARRO *and* CLAUDIUS.]

Varro Calls my lord?   245

Brutus I pray you, sirs, lie in my tent and sleep.
It may be I shall raise you by and by
On business to my brother Cassius.

Varro So please you, we will stand and watch
      your pleasure.

Brutus I will not have it so. Lie down, good sirs.   250
It may be I shall otherwise bethink me.

[VARRO *and* CLAUDIUS *lie down.*]
   Look, Lucius, here's the book I sought for so;
I put it in the pocket of my gown.

---

230. *hence:* leave.

239. *instrument:* in most productions Lucius plays a lute.

241. *knave:* boy (affectionate).

o'erwatched: tired with watching or being on duty.

249. *stand . . . pleasure:* stand by and await your commands.

251. *otherwise bethink me:* change my mind.

Lucius I was sure your lordship did not give it me.

Brutus Bear with me, good boy, I am much for-   255
    getful.
    Canst thou hold up thy heavy eyes awhile,
    And touch thy instrument a strain or two?

Lucius Ay, my lord, an't please you.

Brutus   It does, my boy.
    I trouble thee too much, but thou art willing.

Lucius It is my duty, sir.   260

Brutus I should not urge thy duty past thy might.
    I know young bloods look for a time of rest.

Lucius I have slept, my lord, already.

Brutus It was well done; and thou shalt sleep again;
    I will not hold thee long. If I do live,   265
    I will be good to thee.

[*Music, and a song.* LUCIUS *falls asleep.*]
    This is a sleepy tune. O murd'rous slumber!
    Layest thou thy leaden mace upon my boy,
    That plays thee music? Gentle knave, good night.
    I will not do thee so much wrong to wake thee.   270
    If thou dost nod, thou break'st thy instrument;
    I'll take it from thee; and, good boy, good night.
    Let me see, let me see. Is not the leaf turned down
    Where I left reading? Here it is, I think.

[*Enter the ghost of* CAESAR.]
    How ill this taper burns! Ha! who comes here?   275
    I think it is the weakness of mine eyes
    That shapes this monstrous apparition.
    It comes upon me. Art thou any thing?
    Art thou some god, some angel, or some devil
    That mak'st my blood cold, and my hair to stare?   280
    Speak to me what thou art.

Ghost Thy evil spirit, Brutus.

Brutus   Why com'st thou?

Ghost To tell thee thou shalt see me at Philippi.

Brutus Well; then I shall see thee again?

---

261.   *might:* strength.

262.   *young bloods:* young constitutions.

S.D.   The song usually sung on the stage at this point is "Orpheus with his lute," from *Henry VIII.* Queen Katherine asks for it in that play when she "grows sad with troubles," and it is suitably melancholy. Another appropriate Elizabethan song that has been suggested for Lucius is John Dowland's "Come, Heavy Sleep."

267.   *murd'rous:* resembling death in its effect.

268.   *mace:* Morpheus, Greek god of Dreams carried a leaden staff that caused sleep.

275.   *How ill this taper burns:* common superstition. Lights burned blue or dim in the presence of a ghost.

277.   *apparition:* ghost.

278.   *upon:* toward.

         thing: i.e., material, physical thing.

280.   *stare:* stand up with fear. Cf. Macbeth V.4.10–13:

         The time has been my senses would have cooled

         To hear a night-shriek, and my fell of hair

         Would at a dismal treatise rouse and stir

         As life were in 't.

Ghost Ay, at Philippi.   285

Brutus Why, I will see thee at Philippi then.

[*Exit* GHOST.]
  Now I have taken heart thou vanishest.
  Ill spirit, I would hold more talk with thee.
  Boy! Lucius! Varro! Sirs! Awake!
  Claudius!   290

Lucius The strings, my lord, are false.   291.   *false:* out of tune.

Brutus He thinks he still is at his instrument.
  Lucius, awake!

Lucius My lord?

Brutus Didst thou dream, Lucius, that thou so   295
  criest out?

Lucius My lord, I do not know that I did cry.

Brutus Yes, that thou didst. Didst thou see
  anything?

Lucius Nothing, my lord.

Brutus To sleep again, Lucius. Sirrah Claudius!
  [*to* VARRO] Fellow thou, awake!   300

Varro My lord?

Claudius My lord?

Brutus Why did you so cry out, sirs, in your sleep?

Both Did we, my lord?

Brutus Ay. Saw you anything?

Varro No, my lord, I saw nothing.   305

Claudius   Nor I, my lord.

Brutus Go and commend me to my brother Cassius.
  Bid him set on his powers betimes before,   307.   *betimes:* early in the morning, before me.
  And we will follow.

Both   It shall be done, my lord [*Exeunt.*]

COMMENTARY

The quarrel between Brutus and Cassius is a very short episode in Plutarch's version of the *Life of Brutus*, but Shakespeare clearly understood the dramatic potential in the argument and turned it into one of the most highly acclaimed scenes in all of his plays. The poet Leonard Digges, in a poem included in the Introduction to the 1623 First Folio, mentions the "parlying Romans" and in a longer version of the poem printed in the 1640 edition of Shakespeare's *Poems* writes:

> So have I seene, when Cesar would appeare,
> And on the Stage at half-sword parley were,
> *Brutus* and *Cassius:* Oh how the Audience,
> Were ravish'd, with what wonder they went thence. . . .

Even in the eighteenth and nineteenth centuries when the play *Julius Caesar* was considered by many critics one of Shakespeare's lesser plays, the quarrel scene between Brutus and Cassius was thought to be a shining example of Shakespeare's better work. Samuel Johnson, who did not like the play, called the scene one to be "universally celebrated," and the poet Samuel Taylor Coleridge cited the scene as evidence of Shakespeare's "genius being superhuman."

The inevitable clash between Cassius' cynical realism and Brutus' stubborn idealism not only makes for excellent drama but also brings to light the larger issues of morality and ethics within rebellion. Cassius is well aware that it takes money to maintain an army and it is not always possible to obtain the needed funds in honorable ways. Cassius sees nothing wrong, under the circumstances, with doing whatever is necessary, including overlooking a "nice offence" such as bribery, to secure the money needed to support the men in his army. Instead of viewing Cassius' fundraising activities as necessary evils in a time of war, Brutus, impaired by the blinders of nobility, can only see it as corruption. Later in the scene, Brutus, having just condemned Cassius for obtaining money through extortion, now castigates Cassius for not sharing with him the spoils of his efforts. Ironically, Brutus, accusing Cassius of contaminating "our fingers with base bribes," fails to recognize his own participation in corruption when he insisted the conspirators contaminate their fingers with the blood of the murdered Caesar.

In lines 38–47, Brutus accuses Cassius of being "choleric." Elizabethans believed that emotional stability along with general health depended on a proper balance of four fluids or humours within the body. The four cardinal humours were blood, phlegm, choler (yellow bile), and melancholy (black bile), and it was thought that the mixtures of these elements would determine a person's temperament. A well-proportioned mixture of all four elements would result in a person who was balanced and healthy. However, a person with a predominance of one fluid produced someone who was either sanguine, phlegmatic, choleric, or melancholic. The choleric man, or Cassius in Brutus' opinion, would have been quick to anger, lean, arrogant, ambitious, malicious, and sly.

The argument between the two men disintegrates into an almost pathetic childlike squabble. For the moment, Brutus replaces his stoic nature with one of petulance and becomes a man who torments, intimidates, and belittles the man he calls a friend. Cassius questions Brutus' definition of friendship and suggests that a true friend would not chronicle every fault of that friend only to later "cast" every mistake "into my teeth."

Brutus' arrogance becomes so exaggerated that his declarations become reminiscent of the ones spoken by Caesar right before his death. Just as Caesar referred to himself in terms of an Olympian god in Act III, Brutus, using the same term, takes on the identical tones of pomposity and conceit. Shakespeare continues to draw a parallel between Brutus and Caesar and, at this point, it would be difficult to distinguish one man from the other.

Just as he exposed his chest to the storm in Act I, Cassius now offers his "naked breast" to Brutus' dagger. Just as he bears his chest, Cassius is a man who openly bears his soul. Unlike Brutus, Cassius cannot hide his feelings behind a philosophy. He is "aweary of the world," and his exhaustion comes not only from the efforts on behalf of freedom for Rome but also from constantly trying to prove his love to Brutus. On every occasion, he has foresworn his own better judgment in an effort to placate Brutus. He has done the dirty work required to keep their armies intact and now, Brutus can do nothing but condemn and accuse and place himself above Cassius, declaring superiority both ethically and morally. As the quarrel comes to an end, the once passionate Cassius now appears beaten and forlorn but, as is expected, it is Cassius who swallows his pride and instigates the reconciliation between the two men.

The entrance of the poet into the scene at this moment is more than an episode of comic relief. According to Plutarch, the poet who entered the fray was a cynic philosopher by the name of Marcus Phaonius, but if the actor playing the poet was, as is often speculated, William Shakespeare himself, the scene takes on a more complex meaning. As evidenced in Act III, poets do not prosper in times of civil unrest. Cinna was torn limb from limb and, although this poet walks away with his life, he is insulted and harshly dismissed. The message brought by the poet to the two generals is a simple but powerful one: "Love and be friends." The job of the poet is to uncover truth and beauty, and the truth revealed in this short scene is the importance of love: love between friends, love of country, love of proper ideals. Since the funeral speech, no one has mentioned the love of Rome or the love of freedom. Love between individuals has been replaced with ambition and petty concerns and, as a result, the world is at odds and on the brink of destruction. Instead of listening to the poet however, Brutus labels him an empty, vulgar fool and ignores the most important theme presented in the play: "to love and be friends."

Following the exit of the poet, Brutus reveals that his wife, Portia, has died. According to Plutarch, Portia killed herself by putting hot coals in her mouth, but Shakespeare's description of "swallowing fire" enforces the continuing imagery of destruction by fire. Brutus' stoicism is no more evident than in the telling of his wife's death, but it is possible that his sorrow and grief was the cause of his uncharacteristic show of emotion as he quarreled with Cassius.

Almost as soon as Brutus has told Cassius of Portia's death, Messala enters to report the news of Portia's death to Brutus. The retelling of the information seems an almost unnecessary detail within the scene. Many scholars speculate that Shakespeare revised the play, writing the first telling of Portia's death (lines 147–156)

to replace the second (lines 179–192) in an attempt to avoid making Brutus look totally emotionless, but the printer failed to delete the second passage.

Closer examination, however, might point to the second telling as a way of further revealing Brutus' character. Messala enters the scene accompanied by Titinius. Cassius, still in shock over Portia's demise, verbally laments her death but is quieted by Brutus with, "No more, I pray you." Brutus goes on to deny having any news of Portia, after just telling Cassius of her death and, when Messala tells him of her death, Brutus' response is calm to the point of uncaring. Brutus, always concerned with his public image, could have put on this show of stoic resignation to impress Messala, knowing that word of his response would spread through the camp and, indeed, Messala calls Brutus a great man. By this point, Shakespeare has so merged the characters of Brutus and Caesar that Brutus' words, rather than being just reminiscent of Caesar's words, begin to echo exact thoughts. For example, in Act II, Caesar remarks that "death, a necessary end, / Will come when it will come." Brutus in Act IV declares, "We must die, Messala. / With meditating that she must die once, / I have the patience to endure it now." The retelling of Portia's death, rather than being a compositor's error, allows Shakespeare to continue to thematically metamorphose the two men into one.

Messala also brings the news of the deaths of the senators proscribed by Antony and Octavius. Although Messala reports the death of 100 senators, Brutus has heard of only 70. Again, confusion reigns in war and within the ranks of Brutus' and Cassius' armies. Messala also tells of the death of Cicero. Marc Antony ordered the death of Cicero and, even though Cicero had been one of Octavius' few early supporters, Octavius agreed to list Cicero for death. Knowing he was marked for death, Cicero tried to escape from Italy but the ship in which he was sailing was blown back to shore. Instead of making another attempt to escape, Cicero waited for the soldiers sent to kill him and without further resistance, died at their hands in December of 43 B.C.

The next order of business is the discussion of military strategy. Because Antony and Octavius are known to be advancing towards Phillipi, Brutus suggests that they march their own armies to meet them there.

Cassius, the more experienced soldier, disagrees, arguing logically that if they stay where they are, their soldiers will be rested and better able to do battle. Brutus' ever expanding ego intervenes and he vetoes Cassius' idea saying, "Good reasons must of force give place to better." Brutus behaves dictatorially and his brazen over-confidence makes it more and more difficult to differentiate between the tyranny of the dead Caesar and the tyranny of the living Brutus. Cassius makes a very feeble attempt to speak further on the matter but Brutus refuses to listen. Instead, he emotes on the importance of acting when the moment is right. Ironically, of course, Brutus has yet to ever act at the proper time and Shakespeare's theory holds true that time, and Brutus' relationship to it, remains out of kilter. Brutus himself has become an anachronism.

After everyone leaves the tent, Brutus dons his nightgown and literally transforms himself from his public image into his private self. As with Portia in Act II, when Brutus drops the mask of the stoic politician he becomes a caring, concerned man who can admit mistakes and find humor in his situation. In this very short segment of almost domestic bliss, it becomes obvious that Brutus was much more suited for the pleasures of the home than the perils of politics. In a very real sense, he seems to be a man forced into a role he was not made to play.

Into this short-lived moment of peace comes the ghost of Julius Caesar. The episode, rather than being an invention of Shakespeare's dramatic imagination, is actually taken from Plutarch's record of events. In his accounting, Plutarch relates that the ghost identified itself as Brutus' "evil spirit." There are at least two possible ways of interpreting the appearance of Caesar's ghost. The first would be to portray the ghost as the manifestation of Brutus' troubled mind and guilty conscience. Brutus is exhausted by his angry episode with Cassius and full of grief over the death of Portia. The recent deaths of the senators, the inevitable deaths that will occur in the upcoming battles, and the possibility of his own death cannot be far from Brutus' thoughts. If the ghost were the outward form of Brutus' conscience,

the fact that the ghost identifies itself as evil would be proof that Brutus is, at least subconsciously, aware that the murder of Caesar and the ensuing chaos was immoral. The second interpretation of Caesar's ghost would be as an actual apparition. Both the Romans and the Elizabethans were superstitious people who unequivocally believed in the existence of ghosts. Either interpretation, however, serves to show that Brutus, like Caesar before his death, has become superstitious. It is a fulfillment of Antony's prophecy that Caesar's spirit has "come hot from hell" and it foreshadows the defeat of the republican forces and the death of Brutus at Phillipi.

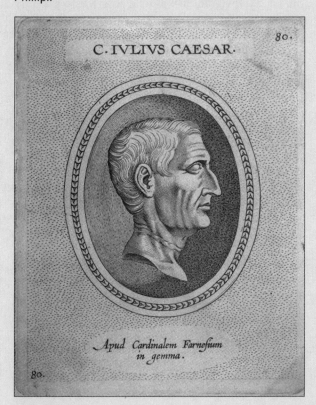

Julius Caesar.
Mary Evans Picture Library

Notes

Notes

JULIUS CAESAR

ACT V

Brutus *O Julius Caesar, thou art mighty yet!*
Thy spirit walks abroad and turns our swords
In our own proper entrails.

Act V, Scene 1

Antony and Octavius and Brutus and Cassius prepare for battle. Brutus and Cassius, feeling that they may lose the war, say their good-byes.

ACT V, SCENE 1
The Plain of Philippi.

[*Enter* OCTAVIUS, ANTONY, *and their army.*]

Octavius Now, Antony, our hopes are answered.
You said the enemy would not come down
But keep the hills and upper regions.
It proves not so. Their battles are at hand;
They mean to warn us at Philippi here,   5
Answering before we do demand of them.

Antony Tut! I am in their bosoms and I know
Wherefore they do it. They could be content
To visit other places, and come down
With fearful bravery, thinking by this face   10
To fasten in our thoughts that they have courage.
But 'tis not so.

[*Enter a messenger.*]

Messenger   Prepare you, generals.
The enemy comes on in gallant show;
Their bloody sign of battle is hung out,
And something to be done immediately.   15

Antony Octavius, lead your battle softly on
Upon the left hand of the even field.

Octavius Upon the right hand. Keep thou the left.

Antony Why do you cross me in this exigent?

Octavius I do not cross you; but I will do so.   20
[*March. Drum. Enter* BRUTUS, CASSIUS, *and their army,*
LUCILIUS, TITINIUS, *and others.*]

Brutus They stand and would have parley.

Cassius Stand fast, Titinius. We must out and talk.

Octavius Mark Antony, shall we give sign of
    battle ?

NOTES

4. *battles:* armies.

5. *warn:* defy, oppose, challenge.

6. *Answering . . . them:* attacking us before we attack them.

7. *in their bosoms:* either (1) I can read their thoughts, or (2) my spies are among them.

8–9. *content . . . places:* would rather be elsewhere.

10. *fearful bravery:* a brave appearance hiding their fear.
     face: show.

13. *gallant show:* splendid array.

14. *bloody sign:* red flag. Shakespeare uses this elsewhere as a sign of battle.

16. *softly:* slowly.

19. *exigent:* emergency.

21. *parley:* conversation.

22. *Stand fast:* hold your forces here.
     out: go forward.

Antony No, Caesar, we will answer on their charge.
Make forth. The generals would have some words.   25

Octavius Stir not until the signal.

Brutus Words before blows. Is it so, countrymen?

Octavius Not that we love words better, as you do.

Brutus Good words are better than bad strokes,
Octavius.

Antony In your bad strokes, Brutus, you give good   30
words;
Witness the hole you made in Caesar's heart,
Crying 'Long live! Hail, Caesar!'

Cassius   Antony,
The posture of your blows are yet unknown;
But for your words, they rob the Hybla bees,
And leave them honeyless.   35

Antony   Not stingless too.

Brutus O yes, and soundless too!
For you have stol'n their buzzing, Antony,
And very wisely threat before you sting.

Antony Villains! you did not so when your vile
daggers
Hacked one another in the sides of Caesar.   40
You showed your teeth like apes, and fawned like
hounds,
And bowed like bondmen, kissing Caesar's feet;
Whilst damned Casca, like a cur, behind
Struck Caesar on the neck. O you flatterers!

Cassius Flatterers? Now Brutus, thank yourself!   45
This tongue had not offended so to-day
If Cassius might have ruled.

Octavius Come, come, the cause! If arguing make
us sweat,
The proof of it will turn to redder drops
Look,   50
I draw a sword against conspirators.
When think you that the sword goes up again?
Never, till Caesar's three-and-thirty wounds

24.   *answer charge:* attack when they do.

25.   *Make forth:* i.e., let us go forward.

33.   *posture:* form or shape.

34.   *Hybla bees:* the bees of Mt. Hybla, in Sicily, were famous for their honey. Cassius refers to the honey of Antony's eloquence in his funeral oration.

48.   *the cause:* i.e., to the business at hand.

49.   *proof:* trial in battle.

52.   *goes up:* is sheathed.

Be well avenged, or till another Caesar
Have added slaughter to the sword of traitors.   55

Brutus Caesar, thou canst not die by traitors'
    hands
Unless thou bring'st them with thee.

Octavius   So I hope.
I was not born to die on Brutus' sword.

Brutus O, if thou wert the noblest of thy strain,
Young man, thou couldst not die more honourable.   60

Cassius A peevish schoolboy, worthless of such
    honour,
Joined with a masker and a reveller!

Antony Old Cassius still.

Octavius   Come, Antony, away!
Defiance, traitors, hurl we in your teeth.
If you dare fight to-day, come to the fields;   65
If not, when you have stomachs.

[*Exeunt* OCTAVIUS, ANTONY, *and army.*]

Cassius Why now blow wind, swell billow, and
    swim bark!
The storm is up, and all is on the hazard.

Brutus Ho, Lucilius! Hark, a word with you.

Lucilius   My lord?   70

[BRUTUS *and* LUCILIUS *talk apart.*]

Cassius Messala.

Messala   What says my general?

Cassius   Messala,
This is my birthday; as this very day
Was Cassius born. Give me thy hand, Messala.
Be thou my witness that against my will
(As Pompey was) am I compelled to set   75
Upon one battle all our liberties.
You know that I held Epicurus strong
And his opinion. Now I change my mind
And partly credit things that do presage.
Coming from Sardis, on our former ensign   80

Two mighty eagles fell; and there they perched,
Gorging and feeding from our soldiers' hands,
Who to Philippi here consorted us.
This morning they are fled away and gone,
And in their steads do ravens, crows, and kites   85
Fly o'er our heads and downward look on us
As we were sickly prey. Their shadows seem
A canopy most fatal, under which
Our army lies, ready to give up the ghost.

Messala Believe not so.   90

Cassius   I but believe it partly;
For I am fresh of spirit and resolved
To meet all perils very constantly.

Brutus Even so Lucilius.

Cassius   Now, most noble Brutus,
The gods to-day stand friendly, that we may,
Lovers in peace, lead on our days to age!   95
But since the affairs of men rest still uncertain,
Let's reason with the worst that may befall.
If we do lose this battle, then is this
The very last time we shall speak together.
What are you then determined to do?   100

Brutus Even by the rule of that philosophy
By which I did blame Cato for the death
Which he did give himself — I know not how,
But I do find it cowardly and vile,
For fear of what might fall, so to prevent   105
The time of life — arming myself with patience
To stay the providence of some high powers
That govern us below.

Cassius   Then, if we lose this battle,
You are contented to be led in triumph
Through the streets of Rome?   110

Brutus No, Cassius, no. Think not, thou noble
    Roman,
That ever Brutus will go bound to Rome.
He bears too great a mind. But this same day
Must end that work the ides of March begun,
And whether we shall meet again I know not.   115

---

83. *consorted us:* accompanied us.

85. *ravens, crows, and kites:* birds proverbially associated with death,

87. *sickly:* sickening, about to die.

92. *constantly:* with fortitude.

93. *Even so Lucilius:* Brutus finishes the conversation he has been having, aside, with Lucilius.

97. *Let's reason with:* let's examine.

101. *that philosophy:* the Stoic philosophy in which suicide was considered cowardly.

102. for Cato's death see note at II.1.295.

105–106. *to prevent / The time of life:* to anticipate the termination of life.

107. *To . . . providence:* to await the judgment.

109. *led in triumph:* led as a captive in the triumphal procession.

Therefore our everlasting farewell take.
For ever and for ever farewell, Cassius!
If we do meet again, why, we shall smile;
If not, why then this parting was well made.

Cassius For ever and for ever farewell, Brutus!   120
If we do meet again, we'll smile indeed;
If not, 'tis true this parting was well made.

Brutus Why then, lead on. O that a man might
   know
The end of this day's business ere it come!
But it sufficeth that the day will end,   125
And then the end is known. Come, ho! Away!

[*Exeunt.*]

COMMENTARY

After the appearance of Ceasar's ghost, Brutus commanded that the armies begin their march toward Phillipi, a major city in the province of Macedonia, located about ten miles north of the Aegean Sea. A small skirmish had actually ensued between the opposing forces of Antony and Octavius and Brutus and Cassius before the battle in this scene takes place. The result was that the armies of the conspiracy, although outnumbered by Antony's and Octavius' army, had commandeered a strategically superior location. Positioned high in the hills, Brutus and Cassius could have been victorious by simply delaying any action while Antony and Octavius' armies tried to exist on the unprotected and swampy plains of the area.

From Octavius' first speech, it becomes clear that Brutus and Cassius have made the characteristically unwise decision to descend from the hills onto the plains and Antony is amazed but thankful at the turn of events. Antony believes that the conspirators are attacking rather than waiting out the progression of events so as not to look cowardly. Based on Antony's conjecture, and the previous examples of Brutus' military acumen, it would not be too difficult to guess who made the decision to move from the hills onto the plains of Phillipi.

Antony gives Octavius orders to fight on the left side of the field, and, in the first overt sign of dissension between the two men, Octavius argues with Antony insisting that he be the one to fight on the left side. Octavius eventually concedes to Antony's command to fight on the left, but he warns Antony that in this matter, "I do not cross you; but I will do so." Indeed, Octavius does keep his word and triumphs over Antony in Shakespeare's telling of *Antony and Cleopatra.*

Brutus' call for "Words before blows" is a tradition more medieval than Roman; in medieval times, it was customary to exchange insults before battle. The tradition allows Shakespeare to establish the animosity between the two sides using verbal rather than physical combat. The task of producing a battle scene on a small stage with a limited number of actors is always difficult. By using verbal assault, rapid action, swift scene changes, and one-on-one combat, Shakespeare is able to create the illusion of a larger battle. The exchange would also entertain an Elizabethan audience with its quick and biting wit.

Octavius hurls threats and insults at Brutus and Cassius and swears he was not meant to die upon Brutus' sword. Brutus replies, "O, if thou wert the noblest of thy strain, / Young man, thou couldst not die more honourable." Even in the face of battle and the very real possibility of death, Brutus' conceit is not humbled. Brutus has, in essence, become Caesar; and Octavius, no longer being referred to as Octavius, has taken the name of Caesar. Indeed, the spirit of Julius Caesar has metaphorically possessed both men, and while his ghost roams the fields of Philippi, Caesar's influence is even more powerful and efficacious in death than it was in life.

Cassius condemns Antony for being like a "peevish school boy" and Antony replies, "Old Cassius still!" However, unlike Brutus, whose character has remained fairly static, Cassius has changed considerably throughout the course of the play. He is no longer the Cassius of Act I. In the beginning, he was a Machiavellian-type character who was able to deviously persuade Brutus to join the conspiracy. Caesar saw him as a dangerous man who observed too much and spent too much time in thought. From his rather cold and calculating introduction, a shrewd but passionate man has emerged. Cassius is a loyal man who treasures his friendships, but because he underestimates his own worth, he, too, often represses his better judgment — and with dire consequences. As he witnesses the imminent failure of the dreams of the conspiracy, Cassius, acknowledging the part his abject silence has played, is consumed with depression.

Throughout the entire play, Cassius consistently bends to the will of Brutus. Watching the death and destruction brought about by Brutus' mistaken judgment must have been very difficult for the more astute Cassius. In a moment of clarity, Cassius is able to observe his own fatal flaw, the suppression of his wisdom to the whims of Brutus, and he can no longer remain silent. Possibly brought on by the stress of battle and a premonition of the inevitable outcome, Cassius finally releases his angry frustration asserting, "Now Brutus, thank yourself! / This tongue had not offended so to-day / If Cassius might have ruled."

As the two opposing forces disperse to begin the battle, Cassius further reveals the many changes that have taken place in his character. He confides to Messala evidence of his discontent with Brutus' decision-making. For the first time, he publicly admits that he is going into this battle against his will, and he fears that the outcome will be devastation for the conspiracy. In opposition to his earlier disbelief in signs and omens, Cassius now dreads the possibly ominous portents of this battle being fought on his birthday. He takes note that the fall of the birds that had followed them to Philippi might well be a sign of impending death. Shakespeare's use of the imagery in the description of the shadows cast by the birds as a "canopy most fatal" foreshadows an apocalyptic ending. Cassius' Epicurean philosophy, the belief that the gods did not meddle in human events, making signs and omens invalid, gives way to a more Stoic position, and Cassius seems to resign himself to his predestined fate.

Cassius is not the only one to change a long-held belief. For Brutus, the idea of suicide is "cowardly and vile" but when weighed in comparison to imprisonment and public humiliation, Brutus swears he will opt for suicide. Again, his own self image is the reason behind his decision. He tells Cassius that Brutus will never "go bound to Rome. / He bears too great a mind."

Both men, sensing their imminent death and the defeat of the conspiracy, say their final good-byes. Despite their differences, they shared a very intense common experience, and they are bound together by circumstance and friendship.

Act V, Scene II

Antony fights with Cassius' men while Octavius battles against the army of Brutus.

ACT V, SCENE 2
The battlefield.

[*Alarum. Enter* BRUTUS *and* MESSALA.]

Brutus Ride, ride, Messala, ride, and give these bills
Unto the legions on the other side. [*Loud alarum.*]
Let them set on at once; for I perceive
But cold demeanour in Octavius' wing,
And sudden push gives them the overthrow.   5
Ride, ride, Messala! Let them all come down.
[*Exeunt.*]

NOTES

S.D. *Alarum:* a conventional signal, on either trumpets or drums, summoning an army to battle.

1. *bills:* orders.

2. *the other side:* the other flank of the army, commanded by Cassius.

4. *cold demeanour:* lack of fighting spirit.

5. *gives . . . overthrow:* i.e., will overthrow them.

6. *Let . . . down:* command the whole army to come down from the heights.

COMMENTARY

The battle has begun. Brutus and his army face off against Octavius and his army while Cassius and his men fight against the forces of Antony. Brutus' men overpower Octavius' men and Brutus sends word of the victory to Cassius. However, instead of moving in to help Cassius defeat Antony, Brutus' men begin a premature victory celebration.

Act V, Scene 3

Cassius' men begin to mutiny when defeat by Antony seems inevitable. Cassius, seeing men storming his camps, sends Titinius to see if the men are friend or foe. Pindarus, mistaking what he sees, tells Cassius that the enemy has captured Titinius. Cassius, despondent over what he perceives as the loss of Titinius and the loss of the war, commits suicide. Brutus sees the body of Cassius and mourns the loss of his friend and prepares for one last battle.

ACT V, SCENE 3
The battlefield.

[*Alarum. Enter* CASSIUS *and* TITINIUS.]

Cassius O look, Titinius, look! The villains fly!
Myself have to mine own turned enemy.
This ensign here of mine was turning back;
I slew the coward and did take it from him.

Titinius O Cassius, Brutus gave the word too early,   5
Who, having some advantage on Octavius,
Took it too eagerly. His soldiers fell to spoil,
Whilst we by Antony are all enclosed.

[*Enter* PINDARUS.]

Pindarus Fly further off, my lord! Fly further off!
Mark Antony is in your tents, my lord.
Fly therefore, noble Cassius, fly far off!   10

Cassius This hill is far enough. Look, look,
      Titinius!
Are those my tents where I perceive the fire?

Titinius They are, my lord.

Cassius   Titinius, if thou lovest me,
Mount thou my horse and hide thy spurs in him   15
Till he have brought thee up to yonder troops
And here again, that I may rest assured
Whether yond troops are friend or enemy.

Titinius I will be here again even with a thought. [*Exit.*]

Cassius Go, Pindarus, get higher on that hill.   20
My sight was ever thick. Regard Titinius,

NOTES

1. *villains:* i.e., his own men.

2. *to mine own:* against my own (men).

3. *ensign:* standard-bearer.

4. *it:* i.e., the standard itself.

5. *the word:* i.e., the word to attack.

7. *spoil:* looting, pillage.

21. *thick:* dim, not clear.

And tell me what thou not'st about the field.

[PINDARUS *goes up*.]
This day I breathed first. Time is come round,
And where I did begin, there shall I end.
My life is run his compass. Sirrah, what news? 25

Pindarus [*Above*.] O my lord!

Cassius What news?

Pindarus [*Above*.] Titinius is enclosed round about
With horsemen that make to him on the spur.
Yet he spurs on. Now they are almost on him. 30
Now Titinius! Now some light. O, he lights too!
He's ta'en. [*Shout*.] And hark! They shout for joy.

Cassius Come down; behold no more.
O coward that I am to live so long
To see my best friend ta'en before my face! 35

[*Enter* PINDARUS *from above*.]
Come hither, sirrah.
In Parthia did I take thee prisoner;
And then I swore thee, saving of thy life,
That whatsoever I did bid thee do,
Thou shouldst attempt it. Come now, keep thine oath. 40
Now be a freeman, and with this good sword,
That ran through Caesar's bowels, search this bosom.
Stand not to answer. Here, take thou the hilts;
And when my face is covered, as 'tis now,
Guide thou the sword. [PINDARUS *stabs him*.] Caesar 45
    thou art revenged
Even with the sword that killed thee. [*Dies*.]
Pindarus. So, I am free; yet would not so have been,
Durst I have done my will. O Cassius!
Far from this country Pindarus shall run,
Where never Roman shall take note of him. [*Exit*.] 50

[*Enter* TITINIUS *and* MESSALA.]

Messala It is but change, Titinius for Octavius
Is overthrown by noble Brutus' power,
As Cassius' legions are by Antony.

Titinius These tidings will well comfort Cassius.

S.D.   *goes up:* Pindarus leaves the main stage and re-appears on the balcony, or upper stage, which then represents "that hill."

23.   *breathed first:* his birthday.

25.   *compass:* come full circle.

29.   *make . . . spur:* i.e., gallop toward him, spurring their horses.

31.   *light:* dismount.

37.   *Parthia:* now Northern Iran.

38.   *swore . . . life:* i.e., I made you take an oath, as a condition of letting you live.

42.   *search:* probe, pierce.

43.   *Stand not:* don't delay.

51.   *change:* i.e., one thing for another.

Messala Where did you leave him?   55

Titinius   All disconsolate,
With Pindarus his bondman, on this hill.

Messala Is not that he that lies upon the ground?

Titinius He lies not like the living. O my heart!

Messala Is not that he?

Titinius   No, this was he Messala,
But Cassius is no more. O setting sun,   60
As in thy red rays thou dost sink to night,
So in his red blood Cassius' day is set!
The sun of Rome is set. Our day is gone;
Clouds, dews, and dangers come; our deeds are done!
Mistrust of my success hath done this deed.   65

Messala Mistrust of good success hath done this
        deed.
O hateful Error, Melancholy's child,
Why dost thou show to the apt thoughts of men
The things that are not? O Error, soon conceived,
Thou never com'st unto a happy birth,   70
But kill'st the mother that engendered thee!

Titinius What, Pindarus! Where art thou,
        Pindarus?

Messala Seek him, Titinius whilst I go to meet
The noble Brutus, thrusting this report
Into his ears. I may say 'thrusting' it,   75
For piercing steel and darts envenomed
Shall be as welcome to the ears of Brutus
As tidings of this sight.

Titinius   Hie you, Messala,
And I will seek for Pindarus the while.

[*Exit* MESSALA.]
Why didst thou send me forth, brave Cassius?   80
Did I not meet thy friends, and did not they
Put on my brows this wreath of victory
And bid me give it thee? Didst thou not hear their
        shouts?

65.   *my success:* the result of my mission.

67.   *Melancholy's child:* i.e., those that are melancholy
are mistaken in their judgment.

68.   *apt:* ready to receive any impression.

71.   *mother:* i.e., the melancholy person who conceived the error.

82.   *wreath:* a laurel wreath.

Alas, thou has misconstrued everything!
But hold thee, take this garland on thy brow.   85
Thy Brutus bid me give it thee, and I
Will do his bidding. Brutus, come apace
And see how I regarded Caius Cassius.
By your leave, gods, This is a Roman's part.
Come, Cassius' sword, and find Titinius' heart.   90

[*Stabs himself and dies.*]

[*Alarum. Enter* BRUTUS, MESSALA, YOUNG CATO,
    STRATO, VOLUMNIUS, *and* LUCILIUS.]

Brutus Where, where, Messala, doth his body lie?

Messala Lo, yonder, and Titinius mourning it.

Brutus Titinius face is upward.

Cato   He is slain.

Brutus O Julius Caesar, thou art mighty yet!
Thy spirit walks abroad and turns our swords   95
In our own proper entrails. [*Low alarums.*]

Cato   Brave Titinius!
Look whe'r he have not crowned dead Cassius.

Brutus Are yet two Romans living such as these?
The last of all the Romans, fare thee well!
It is impossible that ever Rome   100
Should breed thy fellow. Friends, I owe moe tears
To this dead man than you shall see me pay.
I shall find time, Cassius; I shall find time.
Come therefore, and to Thasos send his body.
His funerals shall not be in our camps,   105
Lest it discomfort us. Lucilius, come;
And come, young Cato. Let us to the field.
Labeo and Flavius set our battles on
'Tis three o'clock; and, Romans, yet ere night
We shall try fortune in a second fight. [*Exeunt.*]   110

84. *misconstrued:* with the accent on the second syllable.

88. *regarded:* honored.

89. Titinius asks the gods to allow him to take his life
before the time they have allotted him.

part: role.

96. *own proper:* very own.

97. *whe'r:* whether.

101. *thy fellow:* your equal.

moe: more.

104. *Thasos:* an island near Philippi where Plutarch says
that Cassius was buried.

106. *discomfort us:* dishearten our troops.

108. *battles:* troops.

COMMENTARY

The last few moments of Cassius' life are filled with both irony and a sense of nobility. Ironically, his own men are beginning to show signs of mutiny; Brutus has again given bad military advice, ordering the attack too early; and, instead of joining forces to help Cassius' army defeat Antony, the honorable Brutus' men have begun to loot and pillage the enemy's camp. Cassius, faced with defeat and the continuing fatal mistakes of his friend Brutus, does not back down. Instead, he has rescued his battle flag and killed the coward who tried to abscond with it. Even though Antony is moving closer to Cassius' position, he refuses to retreat any further, and he mourns over what he perceives as the capture of his "best friend." Cassius' final act before his death is to offer freedom to his slave, Pindarus.

One of Cassius' fatal flaws is revealed when he asks Pindarus to relate to him what is happening to Titinius. In an ironic twist, Cassius, who condemned Caesar because of his physical ailments, reveals that his "sight was ever thick." Cassius' shortsightedness has metaphorically and now literally wreaked havoc throughout the entire play. He has been unable to really see what the people of Rome wanted in a leader. He was blind to Brutus' inability to lead the conspiracy, and his blindness will now result in his own death.

Cassius, overcome with melancholy, seems resigned to die, "this day I breathed first." Unseeing or misreading the chain of events, he does not wait for confirmation of Titinius' fate but rather asks Pindarus to assist him in suicide. Early in the play, Cicero noted that, "men may construe things after their own fashion" and now Titinius, almost echoing his words cries, "Alas, thou hast misconstrued everything." It is poetic justice that Cassius is impaled with the very sword that he used to kill Caesar and, as he dies, Cassius calls out to Caesar, giving the impression that perhaps Brutus is not the only member of the conspiracy who has been haunted by the spirit of Caesar. Cassius' death is an unnecessary mistake, but only in dying can Cassius finally escape the bonds of Julius Caesar's power.

Shakespeare again depicts the analogy between the individual and the universe in Titinius' final homage to Cassius. The course of a man's life is metaphorically connected to the course of the sun in a single day, with sunrise being birth and sunset being death. In this speech, the images of the red rays of the sun, with a pun on *son*, are symbolic of the red blood seeping from Cassius' dying body. With Cassius' death, night is come for Rome and the ideals of freedom and liberty that he held dear are thrown into darkness.

Julius Caesar
Mary Evans Picture Library

Titinius is devastated by the death of his friend Cassius. Feeling responsible for Cassius' death, Titinius feels that it was an act of courage to commit suicide rather than live shamefully as the man who caused the death of Cassius. Just like Antony who, proclaiming his love and loyalty to his slain friend, asked to die with the same sword and within the same hour as Caesar, Titinius chooses to take his own life with Cassius' sword.

Finding the bodies of Cassius and Titinius, Brutus proclaims, "O Julius Caesar, thou art mighty yet! / Thy spirit walks abroad and turns our swords / In our own proper entrails." Just as Antony prophesied in Act III, Scene 1, "Caesar's spirit, ranging for revenge, / With Ate by his side" has "come hot from hell."

Reclaiming his Stoic philosophy, Brutus covers up any pain he may actually feel at the loss of Cassius. He proclaims he will cry later and asks that the body not be placed in the camp, lest it upset the troops. Having quickly disposed of the issue of Cassius, Brutus, noting the time as "three o'clock," calls the troops together for one last fight. Just moments before, Titinius had remarked on the setting sun and the red rays of the dying light, so, once again, Brutus has misjudged the time as he drags the remains of his beaten army into the final battle.

Act V, Scene 4

Lucilius, pretending to be Brutus, is captured by Antony and his men. Antony spares his life because of his loyalty to Brutus.

ACT V, SCENE 4
The battlefield.

[*Alarum. Enter* BRUTUS, MESSALA, YOUNG CATO, LUCILIUS, *and* FLAVIUS.]

Brutus Yet, countrymen, O yet hold up your heads!

[*Exit* BRUTUS, MESSALA, *and* FLAVIUS.]

Cato What bastard doth not? Who will go with me?
will proclaim my name about the field.
I am the son of Marcus Cato, ho!
A foe to tyrants, and my country's friend.
I am the son of Marcus Cato, ho!

[*Enter soldiers and fight.*]

Lucilius And I am Brutus, Marcus Brutus I!
Brutus, my country's friend! Know me for Brutus!
[YOUNG CATO *falls.*]
O young and noble Cato, art thou down?
Why, now thou diest as bravely as Titinius,
And may'st be honoured, being Cato's son.

1st Soldier Yield, or thou diest.

Lucilius   Only I yield to die.
There is so much that thou wilt kill me straight.
Kill Brutus, and be honoured in his death.

1st Soldier We must not. A noble prisoner!

[*Enter* ANTONY.]

2nd Soldier Room ho! Tell Antony Brutus is ta'en.

1st Soldier I'll tell the news. Here comes the general.
Brutus is ta'en! Brutus is ta'en, my lord!

Antony Where is he?

Lucilius Safe, Antony; Brutus is safe enough.

5

10

15

20

NOTES

2.   *What bastard:* i.e., who is so low born that. . . .

4.   *Cato:* see note at II.1.295.

S.D.   The actors were accomplished fencers, and the battles dramatically exciting. One of the few contemporary references to the play recalls how the audience was "ravished" by the actors "on the Stage at halfe-sword parley."

7.   Plutarch says that Lucilius impersonated Brutus, apparently in order to draw off the enemy.

12.   *Only . . . die:* I surrender only that I may die.

13.   *so much:* i.e.. Brutus' power is such that he must be killed at once.

I dare assure thee that no enemy
Shall ever take alive the noble Brutus.
The gods defend him from so great a shame!
When you do find him, or alive or dead,
He will be found like Brutus, like himself.   25

Antony This is not Brutus, friend; but, I assure you,
A prize no less in worth. Keep this man safe;
Give him all kindness. I had rather have
Such men my friends than enemies. Go on,
And see whe'r Brutus be alive or dead;   30
And bring us word unto Octavius' tent
How every thing is chanced. [*Exeunt.*]

25. *like himself:* true to himself.

32. *is chanced:* has happened.

COMMENTARY

This scene should be played very quickly and with as much commotion as possible. It is the final battle to be fought before the war is brought to an end, and it should illustrate the Republican commitment to the cause but the futility of the attempt. The action also shows a marked difference between the frenetic activity of Brutus' men and the almost calm confidence of Antony and his soldiers.

Despite the fact that Brutus' decisions have been directly responsible for the downfall of the conspiracy and the death of many soldiers, Brutus' men remain loyal to him and to the cause of the Republic. Just as Portia died trying to live up to the reputation of her father, her younger brother, Marcus Cato, will also die attempting to uphold the family name on behalf of Brutus. In another tactic taken from medieval tradition, Lucilius, a decoy, pretends to be Brutus in an attempt to protect the actual Brutus from being captured in battle. Antony quickly recognizes that this man is not Brutus, but instead of taking Lucilius prisoner, he commands his soldiers to "keep this man safe." Antony knows the fight is all but over and that the death toll needs rise no higher. Just as Caesar forgave many of the men who fought with Pompey, Antony seems ready to do the same.

Act V, Scene 5

Brutus has lost the final battle. To avoid being taken prisoner, Brutus kills himself and Caesar's death is finally avenged. Antony delivers Brutus' eulogy and in an effort to bring reconciliation to Rome, Octavius agrees to pardon the remaining men in Brutus' army.

ACT V, SCENE 5
The battlefield.

[*Enter* BRUTUS, DARDANIUS, CLITUS, STRAW, *and* VOLUMNIUS.]

Brutus Come, poor remains of friends, rest on this
   rock.

Clitus Statilius showed the torchlight; but my lord,
  He came not back. He is or ta'en or slain.

Brutus Sit thee down, Clitus. Slaying is the word.
  It is a deed in fashion. Hark thee, Clitus. [*Whispers.*]   5

Clitus What, I, my lord? No, not for all the world!

Brutus Peace then. No words.

Clitus   I'll rather kill myself.

Brutus Hark thee, Dardanius. [*Whispers.*]

Dardanius   Shall I do such a deed?

Clitus O Dardanius!

Dardanius O Clitus!   10

Clitus What ill request did Brutus make to thee?

Dardanius To kill him, Clitus. Look, he meditates.

Clitus Now is that noble vessel full of grief,
  That it runs over even at his eyes.

Brutus Come hither, good Volumnius. List a word.   15

Volumnius What says my lord?

Brutus   Why this, Volumnius.
  The ghost of Caesar hath appeared to me
  Two several times by night — at Sardis once,
  And this last night here in Philippi fields.
  I know my hour is come.   20

Volumnius   Not so, my lord.

NOTES

1.   *poor remains:* pitiful remains.

2.   *the torchlight:* a detail taken from Plutarch, who recounts how a scout penetrated Cassius' camp, then occupied by Antony, and tried to signal to Brutus' forces.

13.   *vessel:* person, here imagined as filled with tears.

18.   *several:* separate.

Brutus Nay, I am sure it is, Volumnius.
　Thou seest the world, Volumnius, how it goes.
　Our enemies have beat us to the pit.

[*Low alarums.*]
　It is more worthy to leap in ourselves
　Than tarry till they push us. Good Volumnius,　　25
　Thou know'st that we two went to school together.
　Even for that our love of old, I prithee
　Hold thou my sword-hilts whilst I run on it.

Volumnius That's not an office for a friend, my
　　lord. [*Alarums still.*]

Clitus Fly, fly, my lord! There is no tarrying here.　30

Brutus Farewell to you; and you; and you,
　　Volumnius.
　Strato, thou hast been all this while asleep.
　Farewell to thee too, Strato. Countrymen,
　My heart doth joy that yet in all my life
　I found no man but he was true to me.　　35
　I shall have glory by this losing day
　More than Octavius and Mark Antony
　By this vile conquest shall attain unto.
　So fare you well at once; for Brutus' tongue
　Hath almost ended his life's history.　　40
　Night hangs upon mine eyes; my bones would rest,
　That have but laboured to attain this hour.
　[*Alarum. Cry within* 'Fly, fly, fly!']

Clitus Fly, my lord, fly!

Brutus　　　　　　Hence! I will follow.

[*Exeunt* CLITUS, DARDANIUS, *and* VOLUMNIUS.]
　I prithee, Strato, stay thou by thy lord.
　Thou art a fellow of a good respect;　　45
　Thy life hath had some smatch of honour in it.
　Hold then my sword, and turn away thy face
　While I do run upon it. Wilt thou, Strato?

Strato Give me your hand first. Fare you well,
　　my lord.

Brutus Farewell, good Strato. [*Runs on his sword.*]　50
　Caesar, now be still.

23.　*to the pit:* (1) a hole in which an animal is trapped, (2) grave.

29.　*office:* service.

S.D.　*still:* continuing, increasing in intensity.

39.　*at once:* all together.

42.　*That . . . hour:* the line may mean (1) I have striven only to attain this honorable death, or (2) I have experienced only pain in attaining my death.

45.　*respect:* repute.

46.　*smatch:* touch, smack, taste.

I killed not thee with half so good a will. [*Dies.*]

[*Alarum. Retreat. Enter* OCTAVIUS, ANTONY, MESSALA,
LUCILIUS, *and the army.*]

Octavius What man is that?

Messala My master's man. Strato, where is thy master?

Strato Free from the bondage you are in Messala.
The conquerors can but make a fire of him;   55
For Brutus only overcame himself,
And no man else hath honour by his death.

Lucilius So Brutus should be found. I thank thee,
Brutus,
That thou hast proved Lucilius' saying true.

Octavius All that served Brutus, I will entertain   60
them.
Fellow, wilt thou bestow thy time with me?

Strato Ay, if Messala will prefer me to you.

Octavius Do so, good Messala.

Messala How died my master, Strato?

Strato I held the sword, and he did run on it.   65

Messala Octavius, then take him to follow thee,
That did the latest service to my master.

Antony This was the noblest Roman of them all.
All the conspirators save only he
Did what they did in envy of great Caesar;   70
He only, in a general honest thought
And common good to all, made one of them.
His life was gentle, and the elements
So mixed in him that Nature might stand up
And say to all the world, 'This was a man!'   75

Octavius According to his virtue let us use him,
With all respect and rites of burial.
Within my tent his bones to-night shall lie,
Most like a soldier, ordered honourably.
So call the field to rest, and let's away   80
To part the glories of this happy day. [*Exeunt.*]

S.D. *Retreat:* sounded by the trumpets to signal the end of a battle.

55. *make a fire:* cremate.

56. *Brutus only overcame:* only Brutus conquered Brutus.

59. *Lucilius' saying:* at V.4.21–25.

60. *entertain:* take them into my service.

62. *prefer:* recommend.

67. *latest:* last.

71–72. *general . . . all:* i.e., with honorable motives, and for the good of all Romans.

73. *gentle:* in the old sense of noble.

73–74. *elements / So mixed:* qualities so balanced.

76. *use:* treat.

79. *ordered honourably:* treated in an honorable manner.

80. *field:* those in the field of battle, the armies.

81. *part:* share.

COMMENTARY

The last battle is fought. The war is finished. Caesar's death is avenged. Despondent over lost causes and lost friends, Brutus is a "vessel full of grief" whose stoicism no longer comforts him. Finally, Brutus has the time to shed the tears he promised Cassius.

Brutus knows that his options at this point are limited and, as he promised earlier, he chooses to take his own life rather than become a prisoner. Brutus has once again been visited by the ghost of Caesar, and he interprets the second sighting as a sign that his "hour is come." With alarums sounding throughout the scene, a sense of extreme urgency is felt. The arrival of Antony and Octavius is imminent, and Brutus must act quickly if he is to avoid imprisonment.

Even in the face of death and defeat, Brutus is unable to see the reality of his life: "My heart doth joy that yet in all my life / I found no man but he was true to me." Brutus ignores the fact that Cassius manipulated him to entice him to join the conspiracy and Antony undermined his funeral speech and turned all of Rome against him. He also chooses to ignore that these men whom he is asking to help him avoid imprisonment will, with the exception of Strato, fail to do so, running away before they, too, can be caught. Brutus fails to realize that, in the course of this play, the only person who was ever true to him was the man who pardoned him for his allegiance to Pompey and welcomed him with open arms into his home and into his Senate. Julius Caesar, who died under the weight of Brutus' betrayal, was the only man who Brutus could say was actually "true to me."

To the very end of his life, Brutus is concerned with how he will be perceived by the public after his death and where he will be placed in the annals of history. He tells his remaining soldiers, "I shall have glory by this losing day / More than Octavius and Mark Antony / By this vile conquest shall attain unto." His tone is almost boastful and his sense of self-importance sadly misguided. As most men face the end of their lives, they review their own actions and make amends for their own transgressions. Brutus, to the end, lives the unexamined life. He labels Antony's efforts to revenge the death of Caesar as "vile" but he never displays any remorse for the part he played in causing Caesar's death nor does he accept his share of the responsibility for the war that was waged by Antony and Octavius. As he has done his entire life, Brutus tells his "life's history" as he would wish it to read, full of nobility and valiant deeds, but the story history tells of his life is far different. Brutus dies not only a victim of his own sword, but also a victim of his own delusions.

In his eulogy over Brutus' lifeless body, Antony praises Brutus as "the noblest Roman of them all." Words spoken at funerals often ignore the bad and glorify the good, but the last time Antony spoke those words, they were loaded with sarcasm and innuendo, aimed at bringing about the death and destruction of the very man lying before him. Does he now speak those words with the same sarcasm or do his words ring with

JULIUS CÆSAR.

Engraved by Welch from the

ANTIQUE BUST.

Julius Caesar.
Mary Evans Picture Library

truthfulness? Having successfully avenged Caesar's death, perhaps Antony realizes that it is time for Caesar's spirit to rest. It is time for peace to return to Rome. Antony is a politician as well as a soldier and must understand that the only way to truly achieve that peace is to honor and thus forgive (at least publicly) the fallen leader of the conspiracy, paving the way for unity and reconciliation in Rome.

Octavius gives the orders for Brutus' burial, calls an end to the war and sends everyone away, "To part the glories of this happy day." By ending *Julius Caesar* with everyone exiting to tell their own version of the day's events, Shakespeare subtly underlines the way history is often retold to suit the teller. In Shakespeare's time, the Tudor family from which Elizabeth I descended had almost completely rewritten the history of the Plantagenets, the family that ruled England before them, and this theme of history rewritten runs throughout many of Shakespeare's history plays, including *Henry V* and *Richard III*.

Octavius speaks the last words of the play and, in doing so, establishes himself as the dominant figure of authority in the new regime. This new Caesar will become a powerful force in Rome, and his story continues in Shakespeare's telling of *Antony and Cleopatra*.

Notes

Notes

CLIFFSCOMPLETE REVIEW

Use this CliffsComplete Review to gauge what you've learned and to build confidence in your understanding of the original text. After you work through the review questions, the problem-solving exercises, and the suggested activities, you're well on your way to understanding and appreciating the works of William Shakespeare.

IDENTIFY THE QUOTATION

Identify the following quotations by answering these questions:

* Who is the speaker of the quote?
* What does it reveal about the speaker's character?
* What does it tell us about other characters within the play?
* Where does it occur within the play?
* What does it show us about the themes of the play?
* What significant imagery do you see in the quote, and how do these images relate to the overall imagery of the play?

1. Men at some time are masters of their fates.

   The fault dear Brutus, is not in our stars

   But in ourselves, that we are underlings.

2. Let me have men about me that are fat,

   Sleek-headed men, and such as sleep o' nights.

   Yond Cassius has a lean and hungry look.

   He thinks too much. Such men are dangerous.

3. When beggars die there are no comets seen;

   The heavens themselves blaze forth the death of princes.

4. Cowards die many times before their deaths;

   The valiant never taste of death but once.

5. But I am as constant as the Northern Star,

   Of whose true-fixed and resting quality

   There is no fellow in the firmament.

6. Cry 'havoc' and let slip the dogs of war.

7. This was the most unkindest cut of all.

8. There is a tide in the affairs of men

   Which taken at the flood, leads on to fortune;

   Omitted, all the voyage of their life

   Is bound in shallows and in miseries.

9. O Julius Caesar; thou art mighty yet!

   Thy spirit walks abroad and turns our swords

   In our own proper entrails.

10. This was the noblest Roman of them all.

TRUE/FALSE

1. T F The Feast of the Lupercal takes place on the Ides of March.
2. T F Cassius views the Roman people as mindless sheep.

3. T F Cassius uses flattery to persuade Brutus to join the conspiracy.

4. T F Cassius threatens to kill himself if Caesar is crowned king.

5. T F Brutus insists that Antony should be murdered along with Caesar.

6. T F Brutus assures Portia that he will reveal all of his secrets to her.

7. T F Calpurnia and Decius agree that her dream about Caesar is a bad omen.

8. T F Artemidorus pleads to join the conspiracy.

9. T F Brutus is the first to stab Caesar.

10. T F The Second Triumvirate consists of Antony, Octavius, and Pompey.

11. T F Antony and Octavius refuse to have family members murdered.

12. T F Caesar's ghost warns Cassius that he will see him again at Philippi.

13. T F Pindarus assists Cassius in committing suicide.

14. T F Antony refuses to allow a proper burial for Brutus.

15. T F At the end of the play, Octavius emerges as the main leader of the Second Triumvirate.

MULTIPLE CHOICE

1. Marullus and Flavius chastise the crowd for:
   a. drinking in a public place
   b. ignoring Caesar's procession
   c. disregarding Pompey
   d. working on a holiday

2. Calpurnia is married to
   a. Brutus
   b. Cassius
   c. Antony
   d. Caesar

3. After meeting in the storm, Cassius tells the other conspirators to meet him at:
   a. the Forum
   b. the Capitol
   c. Pompey's Porch
   d. The Emporium

4. Brutus bases his decision to assassinate Caesar on
   a. his hatred for Caesar
   b. what Caesar may do if he is crowned king
   c. his own desire to be king
   d. the need to please Cassius

5. Portia is nervous in Act II, Scene 3, because:
   a. Brutus has told her of the plot to kill Caesar.
   b. The wound in her leg is infected.
   c. Lucius has gotten lost.
   d. Ligarius has died.

6. Who means to warn Caesar about the conspiracy with a letter?
   a. the Soothsayer
   b. Portia
   c. Cicero
   d. Artemidorus

7. Brutus offers the crowd one reason for Caesar's death:
   a. He was too sick to rule.
   b. He murdered Pompey.

c. He was ambitious.

d. He was a poor swimmer.

8. In his funeral speech, Antony consistently refers to the conspirators as:

a. guilty men

b. honorable men

c. murderers

d. intelligent men

9. After turning the crowd against the conspirators, Antony joins forces with:

a. Casca

b. Cassius

c. Octavius

d. Pompey's sons

10. In Act IV, the location of the play moves from Italy to:

a. England

b. Malta

c. Asia Minor

d. Greece

11. Brutus accuses Cassius of:

a. being a bad leader

b. killing Portia

c. accepting bribes

d. being a coward

12. Brutus follows the philosophy known as:

a. Idealism

b. Buddhism

c. Stoicism

d. Epicureanism

13. Portia dies when:

a. she is taken prisoner

b. Octavius hunts her down

c. she wounds her thigh

d. she swallows hot coals

14. During the battle at Philippi, Antony and his men fight against the forces of:

a. Cassius

b. Brutus

c. Lepidus

d. Octavius

15. After discovering Cassius' body, Brutus decides to:

a. surrender

b. try to escape

c. commit suicide

d. wage a second battle

FILL IN THE BLANK

1. Shakespeare took much of the story of Julius Caesar from the works of _____.

2. Name two of the ailments Caesar is said to suffer from in Act I: _____ and _____.

3. Casca reports to Cicero that he has seen many strange sights during the evening's storm. Three things that he sees include _____, _____ and _____.

4. Lucius is Brutus' _____.

5. Brutus does not want the conspirators to swear an _____.

6. The job of ensuring that Caesar goes to the Capitol is given to _____.

7. Caesar call himself "constant as _____."

8. The crowd begs Antony to read Caesar's _____.

9. Antony and Octavius, while discussing Lepidus' worth to the new Triumvirate, compare him to an _____.

10. After finding Brutus' body, Antony calls him the "_____ of them all."

DISCUSSION

Use the following questions to generate discussion:

1. A major theme of *Julius Caesar* is that power can corrupt. Using examples from the play prove that this is either true or false.

2. What are the qualities that constitute a good leader? Based on your list of qualities, who was the best leader: Caesar, Brutus or Cassius?

3. Compare and contrast the two women in the play, Portia and Calpurnia.

4. Were Brutus and Cassius and the rest of the conspirators right to kill Caesar? Why?

5. What role does superstition have in the play?

6. Was Brutus an "honorable man?"

7. What might Shakespeare be saying about poets in Act III, Scene 3, and Act IV, Scene 3?

8. In your opinion, is Caesar's apparition a ghost or a figment of Brutus' guilty conscience?

9. What was Cassius' fatal flaw?

10. Should the play be titled *Julius Caesar* or *Marcus Brutus*? Defend your answer.

IDENTIFYING PLAY ELEMENTS

Find examples of the following elements in the text of *Julius Caesar:*

* Puns
* Irony
* Foreshadowing
* Theme
* Imagery
* Symbolism
* Metaphor
* Soliloquy
* Personification
* Anachronism

ACTIVITIES

The following activities can springboard you into further discussions and projects:

1. Write and deliver the speech that Cassius might have given to the mob after Caesar's assassination.

2. Interview someone who lived through the assassination of a political leader. Report to the class the effect the murder had on the individual and on the country.

3. Make a character mask: Choose one character from the play. Next, cut out a mask in the basic shape of the comedy/tragedy masks. Divide the mask in two parts with a line vertically down the center. Using drawings or pictures cut from a magazine, make a collage on the left side of the mask that represents the character's private side. On the right side of the mask, make a collage representing the public side of the character.

4. Write an obituary for any of the characters that die during the course of the play.

5. Create a mock trial: Pretend that the conspirators where caught and brought to trial. Have a third of the class work on the defense while another third works on the prosecution. The remainder of the class will serve as the defendants and the jury.

6. Hot Seat: Choose five or six main characters from the play. Divide the class into groups, with each person in the group assigned one of the chosen characters. Students then break from their "home" group and move into a "character" group. For example, all students assigned Caesar will move into the Caesar group. Each student will then write nonstop for about five minutes an interior dialogue (in first person only) relating the thoughts and feelings of the character. Students then share what they have written within the character group. Next, the students help each other create a minimum of two questions from the perspective of their characters for the characters that are not their own. The Caesar group might come up with a question for Brutus such as, "Why did you betray me?" Students then return to their original "home" groups. Within the "home group," one student at a time takes the "hot seat." The others ask him questions about his or her behavior in the story and he or she must respond as honestly as possible. After five minutes, change the person on the hot seat.

7. Reading Log: For each scene in each act, keep a reading log. The log could consist of a summary of the scene, questions you may have about the scene, new vocabulary words, and lines from the scene that you found particularly interesting.

8. Performance: Pick a scene or monologue from the play. Memorize, rehearse, and perform the scene for your class.

9. Design a set and costumes for a performance of the play.

10. Design and produce a poster that would be used to advertise a production of *Julius Caesar*.

ANSWERS

Identify the Quotation

1. Speaker: Cassius; Person spoken to: Brutus; Location: Act I, Scene 2; Comments: This line shows Cassius as a man of action, one who is willing to create his destiny, not rely on the fates. It also underlines Cassius' envy that he is an "underling" to Caesar.

2. Speaker: Caesar; Person spoken to: Antony; Location: Act I, Scene 2; Comments: As made evident here, Caesar is himself a great observer of men. Politicians prefer men who are "fat" or content, because those who are happy and comfortable will not rebel.

3. Speaker: Calpurnia; Person spoken to: Caesar; Location: Act II, Scene 2; Comments: Calpurnia is trying to convince Caesar not to go to the capitol. There are too many bad signs and omens and Calpurnia is concerned for her husband's safety. She refers to the superstition that the sighting of comets was often connected to the death of leaders.

4. Speaker: Caesar; Person spoken to: Calpurnia; Location: Act II, Scene 2; Comments: Caesar says this in response to Calpurnia's fears for Caesar's life. Knowing that you must die, there is no need to spend your life fearing it.

5. Speaker: Caesar; Person spoken to: Metullus Cimber; Location: Act III, Scene 1; Comments: With these lines, Caesar refuses to listen to Metellus Cimber's pleas on behalf of his brother. The lines boldly illustrate Caesar's growing arrogance.

6. Speaker: Antony; Person spoken to: Caesar's dead body; Location: Act III, Scene 1; Comments: Mark Antony speaks these words over the dead body of Julius Caesar. His grief and anger over the death of his beloved friend move him to seek a harsh revenge.

7. Speaker: Antony; Persons spoken to: the Roman people; Location: Act III, Scene 2; Comments: In his funeral speech, Antony moves the crowd to rage and fury by playing on their greed and sympathy. Here, he shows the bleeding and butchered body of Caesar to the crowds, hoping to rouse their anger towards Brutus.

8. Speaker: Brutus; Person spoken to: Cassius; Location: Act IV, Scene 3; Comments: Brutus and Cassius are discussing the next military moves they are to make against Antony and Octavius. Cassius has suggested that they stay put and wait for their enemies to come to them. Brutus vetoes Cassius' idea and asserts that the time to move is now. Again, Brutus makes the wrong decision while Cassius gives in to the whims of his friend.

9. Speaker: Brutus; Person spoken to: the spirit of Caesar; Location: Act V, Scene 3; Comments: Brutus discovers the body of Cassius. Brutus realizes that even though Caesar's body is dead, his spirit continues to exert an incredible influence over life and events.

10. Speaker: Antony; Location: Act V, Scene 5; Comments: Antony eulogizes over the body of Brutus. Are the words spoken sarcastically as they were in Caesar's oration? Or does Antony say what needs to be heard to bring peace and unity to Rome?

True/False

1. False 2. True 3. True 4. True 5. False 6. True 7. False 8. False 9. False 10. False 11. False 12. False 13. True 14. False 15. True

Multiple Choice

1. c 2. d 3. c 4. b 5. a 6. d 7. c 8. b 9. c 10. c 11. c 12. c 13. d 14. a 15. d

Fill in the Blank

1. Plutarch; 2. Epilepsy, deafness; 3. Lions in the street, men on fire, ghostly women, owls during the day; 4. Servant; 5. Oath of allegiance; 6. Decius; 7. The northern star; 8. Will; 9. Ass; 10. Noblest Roman

Julius Caesar

CLIFFSCOMPLETE RESOURCE CENTER

The learning doesn't need to stop here. CliffsComplete Resource Center shows you the best of the best: great links to information in print, on film, and online. And the following aren't all the great resources available to you; visit www.cliffsnotes.com for tips on reading literature, writing papers, giving presentations, locating other resources, and testing your knowledge.

BOOKS AND MAGAZINES

ASIMOV, ISAAC. *Asimov's Guide to Shakespeare.* New York: Wings Books, 1970.

This book provides an excellent background to the mythological, historical and geographical sources of Shakespeare's plays.

CHARNEY, MAURICE. *Shakespeare's Roman Plays: The Function of Imagery in the Drama.* Cambridge: Harvard University Press, 1961.

Imagery and its role in Shakespeare's Roman plays, including *Julius Caesar,* is explored in depth.

COX, JOHN D. AND DAVID SCOTT KASTAN, eds. *A New History of Early English Drama.* New York: Columbia University Press, 1997.

An intelligent collection of essays on the social and historical context of early English Drama. The chapter on the conditions of performance and publication is invaluable in understanding how modern Shakespeare texts have evolved.

KAHN, COPPELIA. *Roman Shakespeare: Warriors, Wounds and Women.* London: Routledge Press, 1997.

Kahn provides a feminist interpretation to Shakespeare's Roman plays; an interesting look at gender issues in the plays.

NARDO, DON, ed. *Reading on "Julius Caesar."* San Diego: Greenhaven Press, Inc., 1999.

This anthology of essays is an important resource of information on *Julius Caesar.* It includes information about the plot, Shakespeare's sources, character interpretation and themes.

PARSONS, KEITH AND PAMELA MASON, eds. *Shakespeare in Performance.* London: Salamander Books, 1995.

A beautifully illustrated book that explores the performance history of each of Shakespeare's plays.

The Shakespeare Magazine. (Georgetown University, P.O. Box 571006, Washington, D.C. 20057-1006)

Excellent resource for students and teachers of Shakespeare.

SOHMER, STEVE. *Shakespeare's Mystery Play: The Opening of the Globe Theatre 1599.* Manchester and New York: Manchester University Press, 1999.

Sohmer seeks to prove that *Julius Caesar* was the first play performed at the rebuilt Globe in 1599. The book also provides very interesting information on calendar reform and Shakespeare's possible use of the Book of Common Prayer.

WELLS, STANLEY. *Shakespeare: A Life in Drama.* New York and London: W. W. Norton & Co., 1995.

This volume is an important companion to Shakespeare's work, providing both critical analysis and performance history.

INTERNET

The Complete Works of William Shakespeare

www.the-tech.mit.edu:80/Shakespeare/works.html

HTML versions of the complete works of Shakespeare. (Copyright 1995) Provided by The Tech-MIT. Author: Jeremy Hylton

Mr. William Shakespeare and the Internet

www.daphne.palomar.edu/shakespeare/

This is one of the best Shakespeare sites on the Web, providing information on the plays and poems, Shakespeare's life and times, theatre, and criticism. There are educational materials, links to other related sites and a guide to searching for Shakespeare on the Internet. Author: Terry A. Gray

The Shakespeare Classroom

www.jetlink.net/~massij/shakes

This site offers teaching materials and study questions for Shakespeare's plays. Author: JM Massi, Ph.D., Psy.D

Shakespeare's Birthplace Trust

www.shakespeare.org.uk/

Shakespeare's Birthplace Trust is located in Stratford-upon-Avon and oversees the homes associated with Shakespeare, including the house where he was born and Mary Arden's cottage. They also house an excellent library on Shakespeare and offer courses throughout the year. Pictures and descriptions of Shakespeare's homes are offered on this site along with course information and study materials on the plays.

Shakespeare Globe USA

www.shakespeare.uiuc.edu/

A virtual tour of the newly reconstructed Globe Theatre is a highlight of this site. It also offers some very interesting information for teachers and students on Shakespeare, his life and plays. There is a link to John Gielgud reading from *Julius Caesar*.

Electronic Julius Caesar

www.perseus.tufts/edu/jc

Provided by Tufts University, this web site is an excellent resource on the play *Julius Caesar*. In addition to information on Shakespeare's sources, the site includes stage history, character analysis and textual history. Helpful links to other sites.

Gaius Julius Caesar

www.geocities.com/athens/acropolis/2100/caesar/index.html

This site contains a detailed history of Julius Caesar's life and times.

Roman Virtues

www.novaroma.org/via_romana/virtues/html

Part of the Nova Roma Home Page, this site explains the personal and public virtues important to ancient Romans. Author: Flavius Vedius Germanicus, maintained by Patricia Cassia

Julius Caesar: Historical Background

vroma.rhodes.edu/~bmcamanus/caesar.html

An extensive time line for Julius Caesar with many excellent illustrations. Author: Barbara McManus. The College of New Rochelle.

Julius Caesar Web Guide

www.sdcoe.k12.ca.us/score/caesar/caesarwebguide.html

This site offers an overview of the play with some wonderful activities for teaching the play. Author: Joel Sommer Littauer

Globenext

www.50033:shake400@dev99.advanced.org/50033/index.html

Looking at *Julius Caesar* in performance, this site offers director's insights and actor's interpretations of the characters along with historian's perspectives and a teacher's guide.

FILMS

Julius Caesar. USA. 122 mins. B & W. 1953. Directed by: Joseph Mankiewicz. With: Marlon Brando, James Mason, John Gieldgud, Greer Garson and Deborah Kerr.

Julius Caesar. USA. 116 mins. Color. 1970. Directed by: Stuart Burge. With: Charleton Heston, Jason Robards, Richard Chamberlain, Robert Vaughn and Diana Rigg.

Julius Caesar. BBC. 1979. Directed by: Herbert Wise. With: Keith Mitchell, Charles Gray and David Collings.

OTHER MEDIA

Julius Caesar: The Opera. Written by George Frideric Handel

Julius Caesar, unabridged. Caedmon and Harper Collins. Shakespeare Society Productions. Read by: Ralph Richardson and Anthony Quayle and Introductory essay read by Harold Bloom.

CLIFFSCOMPLETE READING GROUP DISCUSSION GUIDE

Use the following questions and topics to enhance your reading group discussions. The discussion can help get you thinking — and hopefully talking — about Shakespeare in a whole new way!

DISCUSSION QUESTIONS

1. Throughout *Julius Caesar,* you can view many of the characters' actions as influenced by choice (or *free will*), influenced by fate (or *destiny*), or influenced by supernatural forces. Which of Brutus' actions seem to come from free will? Which seem to come from destiny? What actions seem influenced by supernatural forces? What about the actions of Caesar? Cassius? Antony? What relationship between free will, destiny, and supernatural forces does Shakespeare suggest?

2. *Julius Caesar* features a large cast of supporting characters. Why did Shakespeare include the characters of Casca? Cinna? Lepidus? Calpurnia? Pindarus? Portia? What do these characters add to the play? How would the play be different if you took away each of these characters?

3. If you were producing a new stage or film version of *Julius Caesar,* how would you cast the role of Julius Caesar? Should the actor playing this role be older (in his 60s or 70s) and weary? Or middle-aged and still energetic and spry? How would you costume him? Does his costume make him look out-of-shape or robust? How does the casting and costuming of Caesar affect the meaning of the entire play?

4. Although many members of Shakespeare's original audience believed in supernatural forces, far fewer modern audience members do. In fact, some recent productions of *Julius Caesar* have cut all supernatural elements (the soothsayer, the storm before Caesar's murder, and so on) from the play in an effort to focus the drama on the changes within the characters' minds. Are the supernatural elements in the play necessary for a modern audience? What are the benefits of cutting supernatural elements from the play? What does the play lose?

5. It has been said that a good leader inspires followers based on a common philosophy or ideal, while a weak leader inspires followers based on the leader's charismatic personality or personal strengths. Given this definition, how good of a leader is Caesar? What about Brutus? Cassius? Antony? Octavius? Which modern political and business leaders inspire followers to work for a common philosophy?

6. Female characters — particularly Portia and Calpurnia — in *Julius Caesar* seem to have a secondary importance in the play, even though many of their opinions are strong and some of their fears become reality. Where in the play are women taken seriously? What are the consequences of other characters disregarding their fear and opinions? What might Shakespeare be saying about the role of women in Roman society? In politics in general?

7. For business and political leaders, public demands can often ruin personal relationships.

Likewise, a leader's personal life can affect his or her ability to publicly lead. What personal relationships are destroyed in *Julius Caesar*? Which public images are destroyed in the play? What might Shakespeare be saying about the relationship between our leaders' public and private lives? Is a balance between public and private life ever possible?

8. Although many of the characters and actions within *Julius Caesar* are rooted in history, successful productions of the play have been set in time periods and locations different from those specified by Shakespeare in his original work. For example, productions of *Julius Caesar* have been set in Nazi Germany, a 1930s Chicago meatpacking factory, and even in outer space. What does the play lose when it's set in a time period different from its historical roots? What does the play gain? What characters, lines, or scenes would need to be cut or rewritten to fit with changes in time period or location?

9. Because the character of Julius Caesar dies so early in the play, some readers and critics have suggested that a more appropriate title for *Julius Caesar* might be *Brutus*. In what way is Brutus' story the focus of *Julius Caesar*? Why might Shakespeare have chosen *Julius Caesar* as the title of the play? How does Caesar influence the half of the play in which he does not appear? Is there a better title for this play?

10. Some productions of *Julius Caesar* cut some of Antony's and Octavius' lines at the end of the play. Other productions cut their final entrance all together and end the play with Brutus' final speech and suicide. How important is Antony and Octavius' final presence to the end of *Julius Caesar*? What are the pros and cons of ending the play with Brutus' suicide? Is the play still a tragedy without Antony and Octavius in the final scene?

Notes

Index

C

M

Notes

Notes

Notes

Notes

Notes

Notes

Notes

Notes

Notes

Notes

Notes

Notes

Notes

Notes

CliffsNotes™

CLIFFSCOMPLETE

Hamlet
Julius Caesar
King Henry IV, Part I
King Lear
Macbeth
The Merchant of Venice
Othello
Romeo and Juliet
The Tempest
Twelfth Night

Look for Other Series in the CliffsNotes Family

LITERATURE NOTES

Absalom, Absalom!
The Aeneid
Agamemnon
Alice in Wonderland
All the King's Men
All the Pretty Horses
All Quiet on Western Front
All's Well & Merry Wives
American Poets of the
    20th Century
American Tragedy
Animal Farm
Anna Karenina
Anthem
Antony and Cleopatra
Aristotle's Ethics
As I Lay Dying
The Assistant
As You Like It
Atlas Shrugged
Autobiography of Ben Franklin
Autobiography of Malcolm X
The Awakening
Babbit
Bartleby & Benito Cereno
The Bean Trees
The Bear
The Bell Jar
Beloved
Beowulf
Billy Budd & Typee
Black Boy
Black Like Me

Bleak House
Bless Me, Ultima
The Bluest Eye & Sula
Brave New World
Brothers Karamazov
Call of Wild & White Fang
Candide
The Canterbury Tales
Catch-22
Catcher in the Rye
The Chosen
Cliffs Notes on the Bible
The Color Purple
Comedy of Errors…
Connecticut Yankee
The Contender
The Count of Monte Cristo
Crime and Punishment
The Crucible
Cry, the Beloved Country
Cyrano de Bergerac
Daisy Miller & Turn…Screw
David Copperfield
Death of a Salesman
The Deerslayer
Diary of Anne Frank
Divine Comedy-I. Inferno
Divine Comedy-II. Purgatorio
Divine Comedy-III. Paradiso
Doctor Faustus
Dr. Jekyll and Mr. Hyde
Don Juan
Don Quixote
Dracula
Emerson's Essays
Emily Dickinson Poems
Emma
Ethan Frome
Euripides' Electra & Medea
The Faerie Queene
Fahrenheit 451
Far from Madding Crowd
A Farewell to Arms
Farewell to Manzanar
Fathers and Sons
Faulkner's Short Stories
Faust Pt. I & Pt. II
The Federalist
Flowers for Algernon
For Whom the Bell Tolls
The Fountainhead
Frankenstein
The French Lieutenant's Woman
The Giver
Glass Menagerie & Streetcar
Go Down, Moses

The Good Earth
Grapes of Wrath
Great Expectations
The Great Gatsby
Greek Classics
Gulliver's Travels
Hamlet
The Handmaid's Tale
Hard Times
Heart of Darkness & Secret Sharer
Hemingway's Short Stories
Henry IV Part 1
Henry IV Part 2
Henry V
House Made of Dawn
The House of the Seven Gables
Huckleberry Finn
I Know Why the Caged Bird Sings
Ibsen's Plays I
Ibsen's Plays II
The Idiot
Idylls of the King
The Iliad
Incidents in the Life of a Slave Girl
Inherit the Wind
Invisible Man
Ivanhoe
Jane Eyre
Joseph Andrews
The Joy Luck Club
Jude the Obscure
Julius Caesar
The Jungle
Kafka's Short Stories
Keats & Shelley
The Killer Angels
King Lear
The Kitchen God's Wife
The Last of the Mohicans
Le Morte Darthur
Leaves of Grass
Les Miserables
A Lesson Before Dying
Light in August
The Light in the Forest
Lord Jim
Lord of the Flies
Lord of the Rings
Lost Horizon
Lysistrata & Other Comedies
Macbeth
Madame Bovary
Main Street
The Mayor of Casterbridge
Measure for Measure
The Merchant of Venice

Middlemarch
A Midsummer-Night's Dream
The Mill on the Floss
Moby-Dick
Moll Flanders
Mrs. Dalloway
Much Ado About Nothing
My Ántonia
Mythology
Narr. …Frederick Douglass
Native Son
New Testament
Night
1984
Notes from Underground
The Odyssey
Oedipus Trilogy
Of Human Bondage
Of Mice and Men
The Old Man and the Sea
Old Testament
Oliver Twist
The Once and Future King
One Day in the Life of
    Ivan Denisovich
One Flew Over Cuckoo's Nest
100 Years of Solitude
O'Neill's Plays
Othello
Our Town
The Outsiders
The Ox-Bow Incident
Paradise Lost
A Passage to India
The Pearl
The Pickwick Papers
The Picture of Dorian Gray
Pilgrim's Progress
The Plague
Plato's Euthyphro…
Plato's The Republic
Poe's Short Stories
A Portrait of the Artist…
The Portrait of a Lady
The Power and the Glory
Pride and Prejudice
The Prince
The Prince and the Pauper
A Raisin in the Sun
The Red Badge of Courage
The Red Pony
The Return of the Native
Richard II
Richard III
The Rise of Silas Lapham
Robinson Crusoe